047950

Leading and Managing Groups in the Outdoors

by K C Ogilvie

Recommended by the
Mountain Leader Training Board

Published by:

NAOE Publications

National Association for Outdoor Education
Publications Secretary Shirley M Payne
89 Standon Crescent, Sheffield S9 1PN

Printed by Sheffield Hallam University Print Unit

First UK Edition 1993

ISBN 1 898555 00 1

Cover Photograph Great Gable from Haystacks by K.C.Ogilvie

Illustrations by Lyn Noble

Graphics on cover by Tim Mackey

Final editing by Shirley M Payne

CONTENTS LIST - LEADING AND MANAGING GROUPS IN THE OUTDOORS

LIST OF DIAGRAMS AND TABLES

******** ******** ******** ********

PREFACE.

Aspirant leaders wishing to take groups sailing, canoeing, hill-walking, skiing, caving or climbing will find any number of handbooks or skill manuals to aid them in acquiring technical knowledge about the activity of their choice. What they will not yet find anywhere in the U.K. under one cover, is a compact volume on the subject of leading, handling and managing a group of people in the outdoors - which is what leaders do for a substantial proportion of their time spent with groups. The reasons for this lack are significant and complex. This seeming neglect is partly to do with attitudes and partly due to the fact that such information is scattered about in a wide range of magazine articles, conference reports, occasional pamphlets and specialist journals.

This essay is an extended version of an article first written twenty years ago. It has been revised from time to time and now attempts to collate some of the relevant material available elsewhere on the subject in order to make it accessible under one cover. One of its purposes is to introduce aspirant leaders in the outdoors to leadership theory and practice by indicating the main themes and sub headings rather than by attempting to cover the subject comprehensively. There is much that could have been included to extend this essay further; the difficulty was knowing where to stop. The earlier version in Langmuir's "Mountaincraft and Leadership" was a treatment of the subject at level one. The present version might be conceived of as grade two. To go further would begin to approach "degree" standard which the majority of leaders do not really need as it would be probably more suited to the specialised needs of the management development trainer.
The intention is to raise levels of awareness about the skills involved in the leading and management of groups of people - an area of outdoor practice that has been neglected over the years.

No claims are made to be fully comprehensive. A thorough coverage of human behaviour would require more than a lifetime of experience and study. We, most of us, only manage to scratch the surface of this vast subject. But scratch it aspirant leaders must if their groups are to have worthwhile experiences.

The script may be repetitious in places but it is necessary. Leadership material is of that sort which attempts to describe the intangible in a system which is open-ended, fluid and infinitely variable. It is therefore less predictable. Human behaviour does not always follow regular logical patterns. It is not always easy to demonstrate the inter-connectivity that exists between different aspects. When the link is one amongst many alternatives, it is often not easy to identify the correct one. So it may be difficult to achieve an appreciation of some of the interrelationships in material of this nature unless links are specifically demonstrated sometimes by being repeated.

Events conjoin to bring the subject of leadership into greater prominence and create a climate more receptive to material on the leadership of groups in the outdoors. The Sports Council issued a Report in August 1991 entitled "Leadership in Outdoor Activities" which spelled out the need for more and better leaders in the outdoors. Outdoor and adventurous activities now feature in the National Curriculum as an option in the P.E Curriculum. National Vocational Qualifications (NVQ's) in the Outdoor Industry, as they come on stream, will tend to give the subject of outdoor leadership a sharpened relevance.

What I have to say about leaders - not leadership - may be somewhat challenging in some quarters in this country (U.K.). I have used "his/her" and "s/he" in an attempt to help break down the gender stereotyping so prevalent in the outdoor world. It causes a bit of awkwardness in composition at times but the device is needful for an area where outdoor leaders are predominantly male.

ACKNOWLEDGEMENTS.

I am most grateful and much indebted to all former staff members of Ghyll Head Outdoor Education Centre over the years whose contributions in discussion helped in the generation of ideas, but in particular to Sue Gillard and Greg Care. Elsewhere and at a later time to Chris Loynes for his very useful suggestions, and to Shirley Payne for her editorial help, hard work and ideas freely given in the final stages of putting this together.
A special thank you goes to Lyn Noble, recently retired Principal of Derbyshire's Whitehall Outdoor Education Centre, for his humorous illustrations. His long experience in outdoor education gives him that insight and feel for situations out-of-doors which gives his artwork a sharpened relevance.

LEADING AND MANAGING GROUPS IN THE OUTDOORS.

Introduction

Although the title of this essay is about the leading of groups in the wide context of the outdoors generally, it will be noticed that some of the detailed descriptive examples illustrating fundamental concepts and principles about leadership have relied, but not exclusively, on those situations in which expedition leaders and leaders of groups in mountains find themselves. This is partly because it is in the nature of these two activities that they are characteristically conducted as group activities, more so perhaps than most other outdoor activities. However it should be no hard matter for a leader interested in some other equally attractive activity such as canoeing, orienteering, caving, sailing or skiing, to pick out the elements which are universally applicable to any leadership situation.

For long enough, ideas about what constitutes a suitable syllabus content for the training of leaders, instructors or coaches of outdoor activities such as canoeing, sailing, caving, skiing and various mountain activities in the U.K. have placed top priority on high standard technical skills practically to the exclusion of all else. But in the context of leadership, where a group of people interacting with each other is involved, high levels of technical skill alone are inadequate. No matter how highly skilled, if a leader does not have the ability to manage properly a relationship with the group and at the same time enable the members of the group to manage their own relationships with each other, then that leader is likely to be less effective. Situations charged with negative emotions caused by poor leadership may become as fraught with potential danger as if the group was unskilled, poorly equipped or out of its depth - which, in a different but very real sense, it would be.

+ It is arguable that a leader with lower level technical skills and higher level leadership skills will do a better job. A leader with higher technical skills and lower inter-personal skills is more motivated to deliver high achievement, but is more likely to end up with an unhappy group. A leader with lower level technical skills and higher level leadership skills, is more motivated to have a group whose morale will be high, but is less likely to deliver a high level of achievement. Much depends on what criteria are used to judge success.

Consistently high levels of achievement and a contented group require a leader to be equally accomplished in both sets of skills.

One of the unavoidable illusions created by any handbook dealing with the technical skills, is the impression of a mass of material sub-divided into watertight compartments, any one of which a leader may be required to recall from time to time. What such handbooks cannot easily convey, is the need for all these items of skill and knowledge to have been so well absorbed that they no longer exist in isolated compartments. It is necessary for them to have meshed with all the others in an integrated manner similar to the way in which tapestry threads interweave to form a pattern or picture. This mingling of threads underlines the fact that each of them has a relationship with all the others. The nature of these interdependent relationships must be understood by the leader for a special reason. When faced by situations, minor or major, requiring particular skills, the interaction of all the influences (e.g. weather, nature of the terrain, group morale, abilities of members of the group, suitability and condition of equipment worn or carried) which bear on the situation should have

taken place in the leader's mind, almost intuitively and spontaneously to the point where the key factors in the situation will have become identified. Identifying the key factors from a mass of background detail is a crucial leadership skill. It is these factors which influence judgements and subsequent decisions. The ability to scan them analytically and quickly to select from the tool-box of skills the appropriate one to deal with a situation, should be an important aim for all aspirant leaders.
This essay does not set out to tell leaders how to "get it all together" so that all that has been learned can be applied exactly in the right sequence, pitched at exactly the right level, delivered at exactly the right moment in the manner most appropriate for a group in the course of a day in the outdoors. Depending on one's experience and point of view, it is either a very simple or a very complex business.

Technical competence in the various outdoor skills and the professional knowledge about the specialised outdoor environments (river, sea, lake, cave, cliff, moor or mountain) pertaining to them that leaders must have, are expertly dealt with elsewhere in other manuals. In the context of this essay they are important not only because they are essential to carrying out the job efficiently, but because research shows that competence and knowledge are key strands in a leader's power base, making authority more credible.

The sections that follow attempt to give some impression of the integrated nature of the task when the job of leading a group is being carried out. They are also concerned with the leader's ability to handle ideas. Ideas are not solid, concrete things like the contents of a rucksack. When the contents of the rucksack are pulled out, they are visible. It is not necessary to imagine what they are or what they look like. If they are damaged, imperfect, too heavy or unsuitable it is fairly obvious. Ideas being of the mind, have to be created by an effort of will. To be able to push ideas around, sort them out, modify them and shape them into some sort of framework that feels right for you, is not easy.

The various concepts and models found in these sections are tools to assist leaders in their thinking about leadership. It is important to be aware that ideas and thinking 'drive' everything else.

"Identifying key factors from a mass of background detail is a crucial leadership skill".

SECTION ONE

AIMS AND VALUES

In pursuing any activity in the outdoors with a group of people, the party leader has one big paradox to resolve - the management of risk ! At first glance this might appear to be a purely technical and practical problem. The leader has to find the right balance between what is dangerous and what is safe. If the leader is engaged in encouraging a novice group to take up an outdoor activity purely as a recreational pastime, the matter may be as simple as that. "Is this white water too technical for the skill level of the group or that cave passage too committing?" As the group becomes more skilled and able, it continues to be a matter of judging whether their skill is equal to the challenge that is contemplated.

But if the leader sees him/herself as working in the sphere of outdoor education, the problem is not quite that simple. Many forms of work with groups in the realm of outdoor education contain an added element which is based on the belief that overcoming challenges, and coping with the element of risk and uncertainty which is attached, is personally developmental for the participant. The straight-forward practical problem of balancing between danger and safety thus becomes overlain with strong ethical or moral overtones. The way this may happen is as follows: what is perceived to be 'dangerous' may be equated with what is seen to be 'exciting' and what is perceived to be 'safe' may be equated with what is seen to be 'dull'. This is then taken a step further. If a session is to be 'developmental' for a student, it appears that it has to be exciting. It is believed that a student has to be extended or stretched by challenge in some way for development to take place. So there may arise the belief that an activity can only be exciting if it is dangerous. If it is safe it will be dull, undemanding and therefore 'non-developmental'. In a nutshell, danger is developmental and safety is not.

This is not necessarily true of course and is admittedly, over-simplifying the situation. But at the heart of the problem of resolving this value conflict, lie the most fundamental questions:

- " Why are you doing it? "
- " What is it all for? "
- " What are you hoping to achieve? "
- " For what overall purpose is the group really being taken out into the mountains, or down a cave , or onto a river? "
- " What is it all about? "

The answer to these questions requires an answer to the hardest of personal questions - **" what am I all about? "** - for it is inevitably the case that the activities of a person with authority over others constitute a projection of that person's personality which extends into spheres of moral activity. A simple illustration will make the meaning of this point clear, as when a leader behaves immorally in seeking to make others like him/herself. This is the likely scenario. A person's concept of what constitutes 'good' is a moral judgement. When a leader decides to take young people into the countryside because " it is 'good' for them" (for whatever reason), this decision will be informed by that leader's belief about what is 'good'. In this instance it is often likely to be a case of, "If it did me 'good' and made me what I am, it must be 'good' for others too." The mistake here is in assuming that the needs of others are exactly like one's own and that all one has to do is repeat one's earlier experiences to create similar effects with others. Knowing about your own values and what 'you are all about' greatly reduces the possibility of trying to mould others in your own image. To do so would be immoral.

unconscious nature of values

To find answers to the question, "what am I all about?", the vast, inner world of ideas, values and aims must be conscientiously explored. It is similar to the thought and energy required to discover the immense, external, physical world of the mountains or the sea. The working model of the world carried inside the head is a complex structure of ideas, impressions, beliefs, attitudes, prejudices, values and working hypotheses which affect all of one's actions and reactions. The process by which this complex of ideas is acquired, is often largely unconscious. Few of these processes operate out of a state of awareness. Many leaders are not likely to be aware that they have chosen many of the values that they hold. They may not be aware that there is a choice and that it is possible to choose which values they will adopt. They may not be aware of what range of choice exists. It is a very useful and revealing exercise for example, for leaders to identify and describe the authority model which they prefer to work under and to describe the style of control they use for preference when vested with authority themselves. Are they similar, or if different, why?

the need for a philosophic basis- the 'why'

Whilst in the past much thought and emphasis has been given to the **'what'** of leadership (technical skills and knowledge etc.), insufficient time has been given to the **'how'** of leadership (processes). Still less time has been given to providing leaders in training with a range of ideas about the **'why'** of leadership (reasons/motives). This could be interpreted as 'brain-washing'. It is crucial to be quite clear here, that the intention would not be to tell leaders what they ought to think, but rather what they ought to think about. It is important that leaders

develop their own philosophic frameworks, but it is unfortunate that they are sometimes left to develop one in isolation, without any assistance from those who direct the work of leaders in training.
Time set aside in training to provide a range of ideas so that a leader does not have to begin this process in a near vacuum would be most beneficial. If future leaders can be made aware that there is a range of choices in these matters about which they have to begin making conscious decisions, they receive a booster start in what is a difficult, essentially self-directed, often very slow, process.

"A booster start in what is a difficult............often very slow process"

It is important to understand why it is vital to develop a philosophy in the leadership context:

the reasons one has for doing things determine the whole way in which they are done.

To illustrate the point, the leader who takes groups out in order to train them to become hill walkers or canoeists, will treat the whole process in a way markedly different from the leader who takes groups out in order to have a different or more informal environment in which to improve working relationships with the group. With the former, "things" are the priority, with the latter, "people" are the main emphasis. These standpoints which favour either 'things' (embodying values to do with achieving a task or aim) or 'people' (embodying values to do with good working relationships) are principal orientations. Leaders need to be aware which orientation is their natural preference or inclination. Without this awareness, leaders will tend to be inflexibly stuck with a particular attitude, unable to move outside it when necessary. For the former leader in the example just given, techniques and proficiency, ascents and achievement will be the main aim and end, whilst for the other leader they will be a means to other ends. The programme of the former will concentrate on the acquisition of proficiency in the skills deemed necessary in the long term for many different types of situations, whilst the second will be concerned only to impart the minimum of skills necessary for the immediate particular situation so that they do not overshadow the main aim of improved relationships. For example, to include capsize drill in a one-off sailing session with a group using dinghies for a problem solving exercise could be a pure waste of time! The way in which the leaders in each situation present the ' content' of the day and conduct it, will be quite different. Leaders need to be aware of how and why they are operating in the way they do, because only then does it become possible for them to see whether style and practice are in harmony with aims.
To be operating in a particular way without knowing why, can be

acceptable sometimes. There are leaders who can work intuitively in this way quite successfully. But it can be a recipe for poor quality leadership. Then leadership practice is likely to become an extension of a leader's own personal motives for pursuing that particular activity. No censure is intended for a leader having such a personal set of motives. Indeed they are a vital element in the generation of his/her motivation to lead others. It would be abnormal if a leader did not possess such "springs for action". But it is important that such reasons are not allowed to impinge upon operations with a group.

Most leaders probably have two sets of motives and aims. The personal set is about what the outdoors means to them. The other set should be more selfless and concerned with what the leader hopes to achieve for and with a group of other people. The act of identifying one's own commitment to one's preferred activity confers certain benefits - only then is it possible to be able to discount or set aside personal aims when leading. Days out which are driven by motives inappropriate for the group, whilst they may not necessarily harm the group in any way, are more prone to unproductive outcomes. Leaders not in touch with themselves may perpetrate acts of selfishness and insensitivity which leave their groups diminished and devastated rather than enlarged and uplifted.

A training which includes a better balance between the 'technical' and 'people' skills will make this less a matter of chance.

<u>personal philosophy changes with time</u>

Once a philosophic basis for leadership has been identified it is important to recognise that it is not static. It can be affected by changing personal circumstances, such as changes in work situation (which may entail different kinds of groups and aims, different equipment, even different activities) or marital status, or parenthood - which brings different perspectives to bear on one's viewpoint. The periodic review and evaluation of aims is a useful habit to acquire. The following brief description of some of the phases to be found in this process are deliberately simplified in order to highlight essentials. It should be noted that the phases do not necessarily occur in the order in which they are described here.

the physical phase

There is a time when the emphasis is on the joyful exploration of new ground both externally (geographically) and internally (physically and mentally). The poet, Wordsworth experienced this:

> "..For nature then
> (The coarser pleasures of my boyish days,
> and their glad animal movements all gone by)
> To me was all in all".

And:

> "...............................the leaping from rock to rock".

It is a time for discovering personal capacities by testing oneself against the environment and great store is set by the satisfactions to be gained from physical achievement, high skill levels and endurance. This is often during youth when physical capacities are at their maximum. But in these days of early retirees, the phase can occur much later on because the opportunity had not presented itself, or was not taken, earlier.

the environmental phase

A deep interest in the environment can develop at any time, but for some people, the time when the pace of life slows down will have a significant effect in this respect. More time becomes available to be interested in other things such as phenomena in the natural environment. Greater interest is found in the flora, fauna and geological aspects and why things are the way they are. Interestingly, Wordsworth found a way via the natural environment of bridging this phase to the social phase:

> " One impulse from a vernal wood can teach you more of man
> Of moral evil and of good than all the sages can."

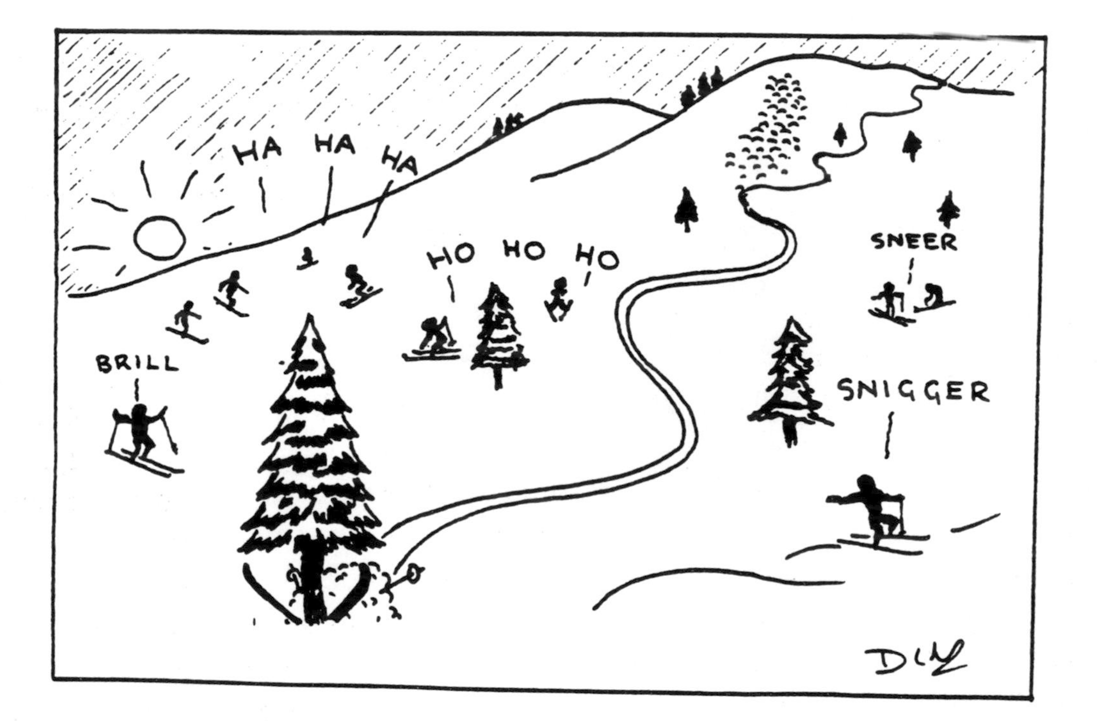

" One impulse from a vernal wood....................................."

__the social phase__

There is some time a realisation that, with groups, the pursuit of the outdoors for its own sake is not necessarily everything and there comes an understanding that:

the effectiveness of work with young people depends more on the quality of the relationships that are formed, than upon the width or depth to which outdoor activities are pursued.

The concern for the needs of the individuals in the group becomes the more dominant focus. It can then matter less to the leader whether it is two or three peaks that are ascended or even if the summit is reached at all. It will be more important that the group is enabled, the modern 'buzz' word is "empowered", to exercise a greater degree of initiative and decision-making in the creation of its own experience rather than implement some plan of the leader.

__fresh outlooks for changing times__

There are leaders whose thinking may not have progressed beyond the stage of, " I got a lot out of it and I hope they will too". Up to a point, that is acceptable, but in pursuing that narrow line exclusively, the group may be denied valuable learning opportunities. This attitude sometimes receives reinforcement from the media which ought to know better, and from less well informed sectors of the community who seem to believe, for example, that leaders only involve groups in activities in order to teach them how to become proficient and therefore safe participants! The dramatic facade of the outward show tends to hypnotise and mislead the lay observer about the true nature of the underlying rationale.

Outdoor practice has greatly changed in range and complexity since the early 1960's. Then, a reaction to the post war austerity years gave rise to a hedonistic outlook which, in the outdoors, was activity oriented in its pursuit of enjoyment. The activity was done purely for its own sake.

Now the greater diversity of types of people participating in some kind of activity outdoors has given rise to a wider range of rationales to support their involvement and there is much less opportunity, or justification, for the simplistic outlooks and single-minded approaches of earlier times.[1] The participants can no longer be described exclusively as 'white, middle-class, able and conformist'.

If leaders have not thought about such philosophical matters, there will be something lacking in the way they approach their groups and their chosen outdoor pursuit. It is emphasised that these ideas will colour and shape all subsequent behaviour in the leading situation. Discussing them with others and exchanging opinions will help, but the final amalgam of ideas must necessarily be a personal act.

paradoxes and value conflicts

In attempting to reach a philosophy about the whys and wherefores of leadership, the aspiring leader will feel the contradictory pressures of a paradox touched on at the start of this section - safety versus danger. The leader will be aware of the weight of opinion emanating from a safety- conscious, over-protective society seeking to impose safety values even more strongly now that we are subject to a Health and Safety Executive. Many safety posters, pamphlets and leaflets, whilst giving much good advice, can act to put the leader in a safety strait jacket. The regulations of Local Education Authorities often reveal an understandable effort to guarantee the safety of pupils by an attempt to seal off all possibility of mishap. This attempt, though understandable, is ultimately unsustainable. No code of practice can possibly envisage all the potentially accident-causing combinations of circumstances that could arise with groups in the natural environment. Parents do have a right to expect that all reasonable care will be taken with their children and that, apart from cuts, bruises, bumps, sneezes and minor fractures, they will be returned to their homes better educated and in one piece. However there has to be a general acceptance that involvement in outdoor challenges may entail some risk and uncertainty. There has to be an awareness that for such activities the total elimination of risk is not feasible and that with such outdoor activities there is the real possibility of either physical or psychological harm despite the fact that all reasonable precautions may have been taken by leaders obliged by law to exercise more than just "reasonable care". There are times when participants have to be dependent upon their own skill and have to take responsibility for their own actions. Because of the nature of the activity situation, the leader will be unable to assist. Even in relatively easy situations it is virtually impossible to intervene to help an individual in the middle of running a rapid, surfing down a wave or perhaps negotiating some awkward section of hillside.

"Apart from cuts, bruises, minor fractures.............
.............better educated"

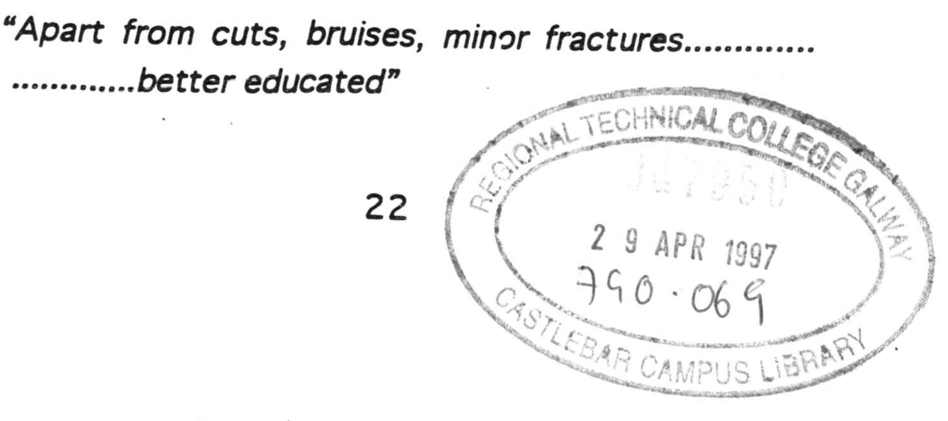

• Countering this whole body of opinion concerned with safety, is another set of values - the ethics and traditions of the various outdoor sports. Many of the basic attractions of these sports have to do with the spice of danger, the calculated risk, testing one's nerve, finding one's limits, venturing into the unknown, freedom and spontaneity. There are other aesthetic attractions of course such as beauty and solitude, but these pose less serious problems for the leader for they are not usually directly at variance with the safety values, though they can sometimes conflict with them. Being with an over-large group, a perennial feature of unsound practice, can reduce the impact of these aesthetic attractions such as peace, solitude, scenery and the impact of the grandeur of the mountain environment or the 'wilderness feel' of a river gorge running through unspoilt countryside.

• The leader then has both a practical and a moral problem in maintaining the right balance between danger and safety. This requires finding the balance between on the one hand, excitement, pleasure, interest, spontaneity, enjoyment and freedom; and on the other hand, too much discipline, regimentation, monotony and the sterile rigidity that comes from over-planning and over-preparation. A leader should always try to be aware if the balance is being tipped in one direction or another - whether towards unjustifiable danger through the leader's arrogant over-confidence or towards too much safety through an anxious lack of self confidence.

A leader has to know when it is permissible to prevent the considerations of safety from intruding too strongly on the party to the point that they detract from the intended experiences.

A leader also has to know when it is necessary for such considerations to be paramount over all others. This is sometimes to do with an appreciation of the limitations of activities. Activities are characterised by their own peculiarities of situation in that the extent to which a leader can safeguard all of a group all of the time, is variable. So, in some situations the consequences of mistakes would be serious, in others, not. For the more serious situation the best a leader may be able to do is provide a structure that ensures the safe conduct of the activity, e.g. a one way traffic circulation system for canoe surfers or skiers will help prevent collisions; a system of signals will help to control a flotilla of boats. Some situations are not immediately dangerous but a potential for disaster is present and some provision of a safety structure becomes necessary such as the need for a ban on unaccompanied swimming whilst at camp.

A leader needs to control the safety factors so that they are a discrete background of good practice working to ensure feelings of excitement, interest, curiosity, exploration, adventure, achievement and a general enjoyment of the outdoors without unnecessary risk.

environmental attitudes and their effect on aims

Traditionally, the safety-danger conflict has seemed to be the chief basic issue for leaders to need to address. But increasing pressures from an ever growing population escaping to the outdoors for a 'fresh air fix' is causing wear and tear on the finite resources of the natural environment on such a scale, that lip service to environmental issues is no longer enough. Environmental concern as an issue must, now more than ever before, be moved up to lie in equal importance alongside safety and danger in the consideration of aims.

A Report issued by the Sports Council in February 1992 called "A Countryside for Sport" highlighted the problem and the implications of unchecked usage of the countryside, the need to plan for what it calls "sustainable participation" and "the long term need to maintain the natural resource". Stated baldly this means that the capacity of the natural environment in the U.K. to cope with the passage of people over it, is finite. The activities of too many people can literally destroy the environment. It goes without saying that if too many of these "participants" are people uncaring about the natural environment, the process is inevitably accelerated.

The traditional attitude of many outdoor users to the environment in regarding it mainly as a kind of playground or testing place for the self, as mentioned earlier in the 'physical phase', can place them in the uncaring category. In adventure or survival courses and even in some types of personal development courses based purely on challenge, the outdoors is also seen as an antagonist to be conquered and overcome because the priority is the benefit that is derived for the individual. Much lower down on the list of priorities is the effect on the environment. Such an exploitive rationale will encourage attitudes which induce the participant to see the environment as a rival or a competitor, as something to be dominated, subjugated to the human will . Competitive or exploitive behaviour has a place in the world but the natural environment has probably reached the point of being the inappropriate place for outdoor participants to practise it. The so-called 'honey-pot' locations are the prime examples. It behoves leaders to adopt new ways of presenting the natural environment to their charges in ways which accentuate the idea of working with rather than against it. The current trend towards minimal impact camping is a start only.

Leaders need to instigate a process to change attitudes by incorporating in their aims and practices, values which embrace the ideas of reverence for, protectiveness towards and harmony with the natural environment [2]. The competitive, exploitive approach too often entails violation and desecration. A desirable shift in aims would be to replace it with the gentler, more respectful, cooperative ethic which would be conducive to reduced wear and tear.

holistic awareness

Leader training schemes do not set out to teach the aspirant how to become infallible. They cannot even give a set of rules and procedures that will work to ensure the right answer in every situation. They can only offer a set of tools and show how these can be used in a general way. How they can be used in other certain specific circumstances can only be learned through experience.

Developing a comprehensive awareness encompassing the group situation, the immediate locale in which it is located and the total outdoor context surrounding it, provides a way towards finding answers to such problems.

Perhaps this point requires an example. At the southern end of Crinkle Crags in Langdale, the descending path becomes a rocky section down the side of a small gully which has to be negotiated to reach the bed of the gully. A leader with a group coming across this 'bad step' obstacle, may feel a need to get out the rope to safeguard movement at this point and could become so engrossed with the technical aspects of the immediate situation to find a belay in order to protect the descent of the people into the gully, as to become oblivious of the wider context. For, above this section is a slope of loose scree. Any other party descending it could send stones into the gully below where members of the leader's group will be standing after they have untied. There is an irony here in that the leader believes s/he is following safe practice in protecting the group by good rope management when in fact, by not waiting until the party above is clear of the scree, or telling those of his/her party below to move to a safer place out of the line of fire, s/he is in fact placing the group in some danger.
With experience it becomes easier for leaders to develop an all-round awareness which enables them to weigh up all the various factors of a problem situation and come up with:

- the right response
- for a particular group
- with a particular job or task to do
- in a specific situation

It should be obvious that the quality of the leader's personal experience is going to be a crucial factor here. Considerable demands may be made on powers of judgement and decision-making. To be effective, these judgements and decisions must be able to call upon a sound foundation of solid, personal, experience.

SECTION TWO

PERSONAL EXPERIENCE

There is no substitute for actual personal experience.

and

There are no short cuts to the gaining of it.

motivation and the quality of experience

If an aspirant leader pursues an activity merely to gain sufficient experience to scrape through some assessment course, then it is necessary for that person to think very deeply about whether or not to continue leading groups. A considerable amount of experience is necessary and if the acquiring of it is going to be regarded as a chore rather than a pleasure, it is suggested that the reasons for being in the training scheme are inadequate and that the enterprise should be abandoned.

The chances of becoming an effective leader are greatly reduced unless a considerable amount of time is spent on accumulating personal experience without a group in tow. Such an acquisition will be adequate when the background of personal experience is sufficiently extensive to enable accurate assessments to be made of most situations and therefore sound decisions regarding action to be taken. These assessments and decisions must subsequently be tempered by knowledge of what a particular group can take or is capable of doing. If it is a new group about which knowledge is less complete or certain, safety margins must be greater.

- Amongst other things this means that:

The leader must be able to distinguish between real and apparent danger. The distinctions are not immediately obvious and some examples will help their recognition.

<u>real danger</u>

A group member would be in a position of real danger in a situation where that person had to rely on his/her own powers because the leader was powerless to help if things went wrong:
For example, if a group was scrambling along a sharp, rocky ridge and the leader was unable to reach one of them in trouble because other members were blocking the only way back, this would be real danger.
A simple matter like running downhill is a situation of real danger. If a person loses control of the rate of descent, a leader will be unable to intervene or assist even if fairly close to the person out of control.
In traversing under crags heavily populated with climbers, there would be a real danger from stone-falls. Canoeists, cavers, sailors and other outdoor sporting enthusiasts will doubtless be able to identify parallel situations of 'real danger' in their own chosen fields.

<u>apparent danger</u>

"Apparent danger" is when a person feels a situation is dangerous though the danger is a lot less than it is perceived to be. An apt illustration would be someone protected by a rope from above whilst descending an awkward few metres of rock in an exposed situation in order to gain easier ground. Fear of falling could cause the person to feel in real danger even when the rope provides security. A canoe novice doing capsize drill for the first time would have similar feelings. Abseiling with the protection of a top rope is another example. Fear of falling on a steep hillside would be unfounded if the angle of the slope

provided enough friction to prevent a slip becoming a fall.
Sometimes leaders make more of a situation than is necessary and end up presenting their groups with an exaggerated impression of a situation which has exactly the opposite effect to what they are trying to achieve. Leaders who attempt to make their own jobs easier or who try too hard to show how caring they are, in trying to settle fears or worries in their groups by dwelling on the hazards and how to cope with them, may heighten the perception, or feeling, of danger rather than reduce it. Inexperience, particularly in the young, renders a person unable to make an accurate assessment of the degree of danger present in the hazards of an actual situation. But youngsters are not idiots and can usually see or feel when a situation is fraught with danger. On entering a cave for example, they may not be able to discern all the elements that make up the danger, they may not be able to tell how serious it is or how to cope with it, but they are aware that it is potentially dangerous. Telling them about claustrophobia beforehand however may not be very helpful. Some people are 'incidents' going around looking for somewhere to happen and well-intentioned advice on what to expect and how to cope may trigger the behaviour one is trying to prevent.
It is very easy to hype up the perception of danger to abnormal proportions. (see section on coaching and supporting)
It is worth considering too, how far such advice in attempting to allay fear and surprise may subtract something desirable, and even vital from the experience. Coping with uncertainty is held to be one of the key assets of this kind of outdoor learning experience.

<u>self knowledge</u>

Leaders also need to know what their own technical strengths and weaknesses are so that they can recognise and avoid situations where they will be more concerned for themselves than the party. Risks taken with parties in such situations are unjustifiable.
Leaders can do much to reduce these "fear for oneself" symptoms by going out and deliberately exposing themselves to unfamiliar

situations. Until a leader has discovered, for example, how it feels to be stuck in a 'stopper', capsized from a canoe in a rapid or from a dinghy in strong winds, lost in a mist or not quite certain of the exact whereabouts (the two are not quite the same thing), there is something quite important lacking in a leader's experience and knowledge about self. Is experience on scree or steep ground sufficiently practised to the point where there are no longer worries about personal ability to cope with the situation? Has a planned bivouac been carried out in order to be better prepared one day for the unexpected, enforced bivouac with a group? Has really foul weather been experienced? All these familiarising experiences enlarge the leader's confidence base and push back the boundaries of the unknown.
Fear of the unknown is one of the prime causes of anxiety. Knowing from experience roughly what to expect in the situations outlined above has helped many a leader through a tough spot.

<u>depth of experience develops judgement</u>

Leaders also need sufficient depth of experience to enable them to recognise those exceptional situations when the text book answer should be disregarded because it is unsuitable to a particular set of circumstances. For example, recommended techniques for descending scree can only be generalisations that will work most of the time. But a time will come when the configuration of a particular scree-shoot, which for some reason you just have to descend, will not allow any of these methods to be used. It then becomes a question of using past experience to help judge what needs doing, what should be guarded against and applying intelligence to the best way of doing it with the means at hand. Mountaineers have a rather vague term for this. They call it having "mountain sense". Mostly it is strongly conscious and insistent, but there are times when it is intuitive and almost subconscious in nature. It probably has its roots in past experience where from a store of minute observations made about conditions, events or people over the years, some detail about the present is different or unique and of acute significance to the present situation.

I remember a day with a group arriving at the summit of High Street in the Lake District. High Street is a very broad ridge 828 metres high with the feel of a high plateau about it. It was a day of darkish haze, of the sort experienced when easterly winds bring air laden with continental, industrial pollution. Whilst having a lunch break the quality of the air around us seemed to be changing. It seemed to become much darker and denser. For no reason I could identify, it suddenly felt 'exposed' and a dangerous place to be in. We hurriedly packed and left the top. Fifteen minutes later we heard a tremendous bang above from the area we had just vacated - lightning had hit it! I had had no prior experience of such conditions. Nor was there any of the sizzling or crackling around metal objects that the books talk about as warning signals.

However, experience, no matter how extensive, is not enough. There are other considerations of a more formal nature to be included in the leader's catalogue of needs which are to do with the actual business of leadership and how it will be conducted.

SECTION THREE

THINKING ABOUT LEADERSHIP.

distinctions to clarify confusion

The term 'leadership' is capable of many widely differing interpretations. The resultant confusion tends to hinder a proper understanding of the subject.
It is important, in this section, to make clear distinctions between :

the leader as a person: how s/he is, or what his/her qualities are.

and:

leadership: which is what the leader has to do and how s/he can do it.

Two or more members constitute a group. When they depend on each other to achieve the group's goal, and in order to do so influence one another, that act of influencing means that leadership exists in the group.
It is only when different kinds of managerial techniques (to be described later) are used to respond sensitively to the people in the group that the leadership function is properly executed - which here is to help a group to enjoy safely the achievement of its agreed aims or objectives.
To make meanings clear, each of these concepts will now be considered

in greater detail.

<u>ideas about leader's power base</u>

People often confuse 'leader' with the term 'leadership' by asking the questions,

- "How do you become a leader?"
  or,
- "Where do leaders get their power from?"

The authority that forms the basis of a leader's influence, is it inherent in that person or acquired, self-assumed or given? The way in which that 'influence' shows itself may or may not be a clue. Some leaders have the power to reward or punish, some have not. Some leaders appear to have a legitimate right to make demands on others whilst other leaders appear to have to cajole, persuade, even bribe to get their way. Classically, leaders influence the followers more than they the leaders, but the reverse is often true also. Leaders are commonly supposed to control events but what are people to think when events patently control leaders at times? They then look at more examples for enlightenment.

A study of the sources of power does not clarify the distinctions to be made between the two concepts, leader and leadership. But knowing about the nature of a power-base helps an understanding of the way leaders with particular sorts of power-bases work and why they might succeed or fail. It also serves to orientate understanding about where outdoor leaders fit into the power-base picture.

<u>genetic</u>

The classic example of confusion is found in the saying "leaders are born, not made". The implication is that those who exercise leadership, do so *naturally* either because of some inherited, privileged position in society (the elder brother or the aristocrat) or because of inherited qualities of personality. It is all a matter of luck and genetic circumstances. Aristotle subscribed to the idea of '*genetic*' or natural leaders in believing that " from the hour of birth, some people are marked out for leadership and others to be led ". This suggested that leaders succeeded by virtue of their inherited traits, through force of personality or because they were highly motivated to become leaders and possessed the necessary energy and charisma.

Max Weber, the German social philosopher, defined charisma as a "quality of individual personality, by virtue of which (the leader) is set apart from ordinary men and treated as though endowed with supernatural, superhuman, or at least specifically exceptional qualities". These traditional opinions are very enduring and contribute in large part to a general misconception that, "You either have it or you don't, and if you don't, there is not much you can do about it". The mistaken implication being that no amount of coaching or training will make any difference to the leadership skill of the trainee. Charismatic leaders inspire and require a high degree of devotion from their followers. Weber also argues that the moral fervour of such leaders is likely to bring them into conflict with traditional morality and normal reason. Such leaders, Adolf Hitler was one although his 'fervour' in the moral sphere was immoral, also tend to by-pass traditional forms of organisation and often display a revolutionary disdain for established procedure. The almost paranoid belief in the rightness of his cause was a factor contributing to his charisma. Some types of charismatic leaders would appear to be eminently unsuitable in the outdoors for the supervision of developing young people! Interestingly, Isobel Hilton in an article "Breaking up is hard to do" in the 'Independent' Newspaper of May 11th 1991 found similar, but less disturbing, parallels in the style and nature of Mrs. Thatcher's leadership. The charismatic kind of person should not be confused with the eccentric character such as Barbara Woodhouse, the dog trainer, or Patrick Moore, the astronomer, who differ in many respects and will often provide memorable leadership and valuable insights.

designated

The leader concept becomes further confused by the fact that some people such as headteachers, directors of nursing or foremen are appointed leader roles without the benefit of leadership training, when authority, higher up the hierarchy chain, invests them with power to exert influence over others lower in the chain. They are not natural but '*designated* ' leaders who may, or may not, be adequate leaders. The criteria, one of which might be the idea of 'seniority', governing the process of their selection may have very little to do with their leadership ability. Reference by subordinates and others to such people can often be derisory or cynical and they are seen as having been "promoted to a higher level of inefficiency". Derisory or not, there may well be grains of truth there. Being good at the respective jobs of teaching or doctoring does not necessarily mean that a person will make a good headteacher or a hospital manager. Nevertheless, those so designated have responsibility and power by virtue of the position or office they hold, and are, or should be, accountable for the exercise of it.

selected

Pre World War 2, officers in the Armed Services often fell within the 'designated' category. But now their appointment is characterised by a rigorous process of *selection* to identify those with the qualities deemed to make the best leaders for the requirements of military situations. These qualities are seen as natural leadership traits which are then developed by further training. This is a process of selection based on a kind of merit or worth which differs from working skill. But it is important to note that though the Armed Services believe they are selecting the "best" leaders - and for their purposes they are, it is necessary to pose the question, "Best for what ?" There is no leader who is 'best', in an absolute sense, for all circumstances.

elected

A further category of people such as M.P.s, Chairpersons and Shop

Stewards are '*elected*'. They earn their positions because of some worth which is perceived by those electing them. It may be their career history or their achievements or their personal charismatic qualities that are the important factors here. It is thus a worth or ability that may not necessarily be relevant to a leadership role. Their tenure of office will depend on the maintenance of that perceived worth or the popularity of decisions made - neither of which needs necessarily to be underwritten by sound leadership. However, you cannot fool all of the people all of the time, and the leader who would be long-lived needs to keep this in mind!

contingent

Contingencies tend to throw up leaders so we may call these '*contingent*' leaders. Leadership is sometimes seen to be vested in, or arise from, a person having the specialist knowledge or skill to solve the problems presented by particular circumstances. A qualified first-aider coming upon the scene of a vehicle collision will be able to enlist and coordinate the assistance of those standing around who do not know what to do. However, attempts to order them about after the emergency is over will be resented and resisted. The classic example of Winston Churchill's elevation to power at the start of World War Two might be seen simply as contingent, but is not. It was his qualities and personality that fitted the situation rather than his skills and knowledge. At the risk of causing confusion, we might call this charismatic-contingent. So here there is a blurring of the classifications which is a timely warning against being too ready to stereotype leaders into single categories.

Sometimes it is **any** person whose skills and knowledge render them most able to satisfy the needs, wants or ambitions of the group members at a particular time. It is not always the 'designated' leader upon whom this contingent mantle falls and this can cause anxieties about status and over-sharp reactions in those designated leaders unprepared for the appearance of this phenomenon. Leaders need to be

aware that leadership can move around the members of a group. A group member voicing what everyone feels at the time, is taking a leadership initiative and may not even be aware that that is what s/he is doing.
Leaders need to be aware when the initiative is with them and when it is not and they need to be aware when it needs be with them and when it does not.
Contingent leaders labour under the disadvantage that they are rarely able to operate outside the very limited range of conditions contained in the circumstances that gave them power. Churchill and the Tory party's displacement from power at the end of World War Two has a contingent feel about it.

outdoor leaders

Leaders of groups in the outdoors are different in being essentially *self appointed* in the sense that they are not designated or elected in the first place by others. Outdoor activity leaders (or outdoor educationists, if that is preferable) tend to come to their leading through a belief that taking groups out into the hills or onto the water is a good thing. They are primarily self motivated. They have come voluntarily to be in this situation so may be assumed to be well motivated too - a prerequisite in any leader. Their previous outdoor experience gives their power base a 'contingent feel' which will require to be complemented substantially (and legitimised), usually by formal training, in order to escape the restricting limitations of the contingent leader and to attain the wider, flexible and more dynamic perspective provided by modern leadership theory and practice.

The outdoor leadership situation has other noteworthy and different features.
In industrial situations, the group process is used as a means to give a team a competitive edge in the achievement of its ends, task or goal.
The work of the outdoor leader is unique in that the process of group interaction and cooperation itself is often the task in order to facilitate the personal and social growth of the members in the group.

And whilst the group is often competing against the environment or itself, it is not usually competing against others.

"And whilst the group is often competing against the environment or itself, it is not usually competing against others"

The outdoor situation is also distinctive in that compared to a gamut of situations researched by authorities on leadership, the outdoor leader is usually an older, adult person leading a group of younger people. S/he is not normally part of a peer group, a project team or a firm of colleagues as in a business. So age is recognisable here as a component of the leader's authority. This gives it a 'parental' complexion which is also recognised and supported by law which regards adult leaders of the young as acting 'in loco parentis', i.e. in the place of a parent, and they even have to take more than the reasonable care a parent would take. This legal imperative may be felt to put the use of power-sharing methods characteristic of some leadership styles under some handicap and difficulty.

Being the adult amongst younger ones also gives the outdoor leader's experience, skill and knowledge of the outdoors a greater prominence. It is very obvious where the technical expertise lies in the group. Together, age and expertise combine to give the adult a status in the group which will make any exercise of power sharing a more complicated business. With ten to twelve year olds all that is needed to harness their enthusiasm is the power of suggestion and a kind of enlightened despotic parentalism. With teenagers going through all the anti-authority trauma there is much more work to be done to achieve credibility.

roles-behaviours-skills

The fore-going brief review is useful in showing how concepts of leadership have become blurred by too close an association with the various ways that people become leaders. One is erroneously taken to be synonymous with the other.

There are thus clear distinctions to be made between the concepts of 'leader' and 'leadership'.

• The **leader** is a person exercising a definite and particular role in relation to others. A **role** is a set of expected behaviours associated with a position in a group - the role of a follower might be to listen and obey, for example. There are other kinds of roles seen in groups which will be looked at later.

• **Leadership** is a set of identifiable behaviours and functions which is used, not only by the leader, but sometimes by other individuals in the group, which are intended to influence the others in order to achieve particular aims or goals. Within these sets of behaviours it is possible to identify particular ***skills which can be acquired through training*** - of which more will be said later. But before moving onto those behaviours and skills, it will be useful to look closely at other attributes associated with the leader.

leader qualities

"Leaders are neither born nor made - they grow" [3]. Whilst the acquisition and possession of leadership skills may be a prerequisite for effective leading, they do not result in "instant leadership" . Those skills by themselves however, will be insufficient unless a range of particular personal qualities are present to drive them. It is these qualities which give colour and substance to the quality of maturity possessed by a person. The degree of acquired wisdom and personal maturity, which is not necessarily dependent on age, is closely linked with the extent to which a person may be effective as a leader.
The manner in which qualities are shown, varies greatly in people. It is the way in which a quality is used by a person which gives it either a good or a bad characteristic. The courage, tenacity and single-mindedness in Winston Churchill during the period 1940-45 was admirable and totally suited to the times, but the tenacity and single-mindedness of Margaret Thatcher in the 1980s was ambivalently received. Clearly, qualities are coloured by a person's set of values and beliefs and are even affected by their behavioural habits. Qualities in leaders thus come in mixtures of the good which may help, and the bad which may hinder. Amongst the qualities which might be seen as more desirable in a leader are warmth, enthusiasm, courage (both physical and moral), integrity, patience and humility. Higher key qualities would be competency and potency (see below). But any quality displayed or used excessively can be a mixed blessing.

competency
Here competency is of a general nature almost related to outlook, unlike a more specific competency which applies to a particular skill. It is of that basic kind in which a person is neither inhibited by past precedents, traditions or past mistakes, nor is deterred by fears of failure or pessimism about the future, but who deals freely and effectively with the present here and now.

potency
Potency is held to be that crucial quality derived from the development of the other qualities and which links style (see below) and skill. It is the capacity to be powerful appropriately to the circumstances and people of a particular situation; to be assertive without being aggressive. It is the capacity to cope confidently with uncertainty and the unknown - which for outdoor leaders is probably the most important test of all. The most effective leader is one who is experienced by a group as being potent.

more qualities for outdoor leaders
Because the outdoor leader's situation has special characteristics and particular differences (see earlier sub-section) there are certain qualities or attributes of personality that might be deemed as more advantageous for such leaders to possess.
Enthusiasm has already been mentioned. Its presence could be expected in a self-motivated person, but the ability to transmit this feeling and 'infect' others with it, is perhaps essential to those leading the young. Enthusiasm is one way of raising levels of motivation in others. Enthusiasm is particularly useful if combined with empathy when the youngsters are innocent volunteers and especially if their morale needs to be lifted when conditions deteriorate to become hard, miserable, or uncomfortable. But it should be noted that insensitive enthusiasm feels like a steam-roller !
Allied with enthusiasm, is a sense of humour, the capacity to be humorous and the ability to inject humour into learning situations. It is

difficult to decide whether a capacity to be humorous is a quality or a skill - the one seems to blend so subtly into the other that the boundaries between capacity and ability are quite indistinct. It is certain that skill with humour can be acquired and improved upon with practice, but there does seem to need to be some underlying, inherent prerequisite for a person not only to see what is funny in a situation but also make humour out of it as the cartoonists do. There is no better way to overcome the moodiness, the apathy, or the negative attitudes that are sometimes found in teenagers. A skillful combination of enthusiasm and humour can come close to being charismatic.

It is important to distinguish between being funny, acting the clown and providing fun however. People sometimes think they are being funny by taking a rise out of others and calling it a joke. The wise leader will avoid committing this type of error. In groups, the practice of making jokes at someone else's expense should be discouraged. Any joke that has to be paid for by someone's discomfiture can lead to undesirable repercussions which have a disquieting habit of occurring at the most inopportune moments.

Clowning around can be a useful tool for the leader. With some groups it can make him/her appear more human or approachable, less of a stuffy adult - it is a means of breaking down barriers. With the wrong sort of group it would have the opposite effect. Providing it is not overused to the extent that a group ceases to take him/her seriously, and providing it is used with discrimination, acting the clown can help relationships. Some of the things that leaders have to do are not very interesting for young people. Induction processes, briefings, safety preparations, the checking of gear for example, may all be a bit dull. In these kinds of situation, the ability to think "laterally" can sometimes be a way of lightening the heavy stuff or even introducing a feeling of fun. If the conventional can be given the appearance of the unconventional or unusual, it often jerks people out of the 'hypnosis of routine' in such a way as is likely to intrigue and hold the interest. The use of cartoons in this book sometimes emphasises a point in a lateral way.

Any of the above-mentioned qualities can cause a leader to be regarded as 'a bit of a character', someone who is 'off-beat' and whose company is stimulating. With such people the occurrence of possible problems with leader-group relationships is greatly diminished.

personal style

The unconscious or intuitive manner in which a person combines personal qualities with the range of leader skills is uniquely distinctive to that person and is the personal style of his/her leadership. It will tend to be this way until the person begins consciously to think about it. The person is locked into a particular kind of leading behaviour because of an unawareness of other alternatives. Sometimes the personal style will suit the situation, sometimes it will not. Leaders need to be able to escape from their preferred or natural style by having available alternatives.

The use of the word "style" here denotes the unique manner in which a person leads. It is partly derived from an inner state of 'being' - it is subjective and personal.

" Style " is used later as a term to portray distinct, identifiable ways of leading which are objective and exist in their own abstract rights. The different styles can be consciously chosen and adopted to suit appropriate circumstances.

A leader can do much to acquire a wider range of leading behaviours and skills. Conscientious leaders will find that there is as much material here as there is on the technical aspects of their preferred outdoor activity.

The cultural traditions of Britain seem to have been less fertile ground for this body of knowledge. There seems to have been a general resistance to its acceptance, growth and development, particularly in the outdoors. Preoccupation with the technical aspects of an activity, and fears that any 'digressions' would result in "a fall in standards" seem to be elements contributing to this stance. The 1980s saw a welcome waning of this attitude. The world of industry and commerce,

in beginning to appreciate the value of managers having good relationship skills and a variety of leading styles, seems to have precipitated a growth in management training courses. The school curriculum has acknowledged the importance of personal and social education. Some of the content of leadership training, such as the understanding of self and others, is to be found in both of these areas.
It is sometimes not appreciated that the processes of managing, teaching and leading are very similar in the skills and the knowledge about people that each requires.

It is only when technical skills are used equally in combination with leader skills and relationship skills that effective leadership can happen consistently.

SECTION FOUR

LEADERSHIP MODELS AND LEADERSHIP STYLES

five elements to consider

In looking at leadership models and styles it may help to keep in mind throughout that up to five main elements may be involved. In the models which are described, some or all of these features may be present. In no particular order they are;

- the task:- some aim or goal that will be done or is being done.
- the group:- considered as a whole.
- the individual:- considered as a person in his/her own right or as a part of the group.
- the environment:- terrain or weather.
- situational conditions:- other special conditions prevailing.

A number of ' models ' about leadership have been propounded. They are regarded as significant in the development of thought about leadership training but have only become more generally known in the outdoors world since the middle to late 1970s. They are very helpful and useful but should only be used as aids to help leaders to think and develop their own ideas about leadership. They should not be regarded as tablets of stone about leadership. These thinking devices are essential for the formulating and honing of a personal conceptual framework of

ideas.
This section looks at four leadership models. Also included is a model about groups. It seemed needful since leaders are as nothing without them. The risk of confusing the reader with too many models is taken because one of many models is more likely to "press a button of comprehension", whilst too few may reduce the "success rate" of dawning enlightenment.

action centred leadership - John Adair [4]

This model conceives of three main aspects that a leader will have to keep in mind continually and cope with if a particular task or goal is to be achieved.

Diagram 1. - Adair's three circle action-centred leadership.

All three areas should be regarded as interlinked in that an over concentration on one will be to the detriment of the other two.
If the needs of the task are made paramount to the extent that the needs of individuals or the team are ignored or overridden for too long, it is less likely that the task will be achieved. A single-minded concentration by the leader on the task is likely to result in a breakdown of communication with the group. Also possible is the

" A single-minded concentration by the leader on the task is likely to result in a breakdown in communication"

alienation of some or all of its members and the loss of their willing cooperation in the achievement of the goal. Trying to push on when the group needs a rest, or a stop to eat, or when someone has developed a bad blister would be typical examples of this kind of situation. Unless the leader has a very good reason for wanting to push on and can convince or persuade the whole group of the rightness of the case, the situation will eventually grind to a halt until the neglected element is given its due consideration and dealt with.
Conversely, concentrating too much on individuals in the group could mean that the attainment of the goal is put in jeopardy or never achieved.

This model is comprehensive in its visualisation of the scope of leadership tasks. It is dynamic in providing a way for a leader to sustain leadership in a variety of different situations.
The model also provides one way for a leader to identify and decide which of the three areas most requires immediate attention in a working situation.
It can also work on the "fly in the ointment" principle by visualising the three circles as pots of ointment any one of which, at any time, is likely to have a fly in it that needs to be removed!
You could also use this model to decide the long term priority area of your focus when setting up a particular expedition.

In the context of the 1990s however and the greater concern about the state of the natural environment, (see section one and 'environmental attitudes') it would seem appropriate to make this model into the shape of a four-leafed clover by adding another circle to take account of the needs of the environment.

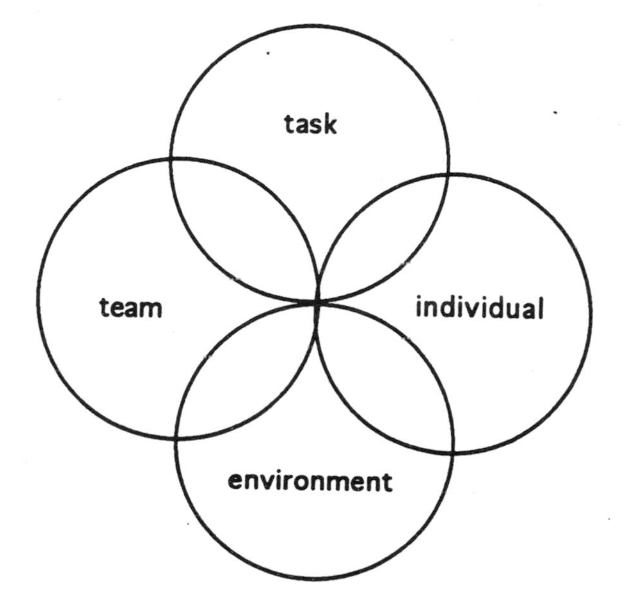

Diagram 2. - Adair's three circles environmentally amended to four.

The impact of recreational and educational users of the countryside is everywhere increasingly apparent. The scars of footpath erosion, the destruction of sensitive sites, the over use of particular places for popular activities are examples of a growing need for leaders to temper their usage patterns with discretion and consider equally viable alternatives[1].

<u>needs of task/individual/group</u>

The description of this model is not complete without the list of the needs of the task, the individual and the group referred to in the diagram1. above. They are included here for convenience and completeness:

Task needs

Define the task.
Make a plan.
Have competence in all skill areas.
Have necessary equipment.
Give information/teach skills.
Allocate work and resources.
Control pace/maintain standards.
Check performance against plans.
Adjust plan as needed.
Bring it to a close.

Individual needs [5]

In order of importance, with the most immediate first:
Physical:food, water, sleep, shelter, warm and dry.
Safety:feel safe and secure.
Social:feel liked and belonging.
Self-esteem:status and recognition of worth.
Sense of identity:purpose, achievement, have values.

(The leader needs to be aware of, know about, understand, recognise, encourage and make allowances for these needs in the group.)

Group needs

Plan group composition.
Encourage participation/motivation.
Set standards.
Maintain discipline.
Facilitate communication.
Build team spirit, cohesion and trust.
Resolve interpersonal differences and conflicts.
Relieve tension.
Build group morale.
Train the group.
Co-ordinate group activities.

control and power - Tannenbaum and Schmidt [6]

This is a useful model for looking at the different ways a leader can handle power and control in a group.

TELLS	SELLS	TESTS	CONSULTS	JOINS	DELEGATES
	Leader	retains		control	
		Leader	shares		control

Diagram 3. - Tannenbaum and Schmidt's continuum of Control and Power.

It sees leadership as a variety of roles lying in a range between two extremes. At one end is maximum intervention - as by a dictator who asks all the questions, gives all the answers, makes all the decisions and gives all the orders. At the other extreme there is a minimum of intervention - as when delegating jobs to others. As one moves further up the line in the diagram: 3, the leader progressively decides, or should do, to give up more actual control whilst the people in the group receive more responsibility and therefore more power/control over what is happening. The leader has to decide which particular style is the more appropriate for the situation.
This model emphasises the idea that leadership is an interactive, two-way process. As the relationship between the leader and the group develops it becomes possible, sometimes necessary or desirable, for the leader to use alternative ways of exercising power.

At times the group's reaction to the leader will determine what style is adopted. At other times, because situations can change so rapidly from moment to moment, it might be the nature of a particular situation which is the deciding factor. Although leaders may have a preferred style that is a reflection of their personality and comes naturally, it will not always be the appropriate style to use in particular circumstances. It is very important to be able to "mix and match" to suit circumstances. An inability to be flexible with regard to the style of leadership that might be best suited to a situation, would be a serious limitation on a leader's effectiveness, credibility and possibly tenure of office.
Thus a number of useful options are demonstrated in this model. They should not be regarded as fixed entities in any way but as part of a continuum where one element fuses imperceptibly into the next.

A brief explanatory note about the various alternatives may be useful.

tells
The leader assesses the situation, the group and the resources

available, selects a course of action and tells the group what to do. Reasons may or may not be given. "This is how it is going to be and this is how we will do it".

<u>sells</u>
The leader chooses a course of action as before but this time gives reasons and explanations to highlight the advantages of the plan and to persuade the group about its rightness. " I want you to do this because......., so that....".

<u>tests</u>
The leader identifies and outlines the problem or situation giving some of the relevant background information and possible options. There will be some discussion but it will be confined to answering objections rather than an open-ended debate before going ahead with the intended course of action. " How do you feel about it ?."

<u>consults</u>
The leader presents the problem and background thinking as before but then asks the group for ideas and comments with the possibility that the intended decision may or may not be modified. The leader reserves the right to impose his/her own decision. " What do you think - any comments?".

<u>joins</u>
The leader presents the problem and perhaps some of the relevant background information and thinking together with some suggestions for possible solutions. The leader then asks for ideas and help and joins the group. The final decision is likely to be a consensus, a joint one-the result of a real sharing and exchange of views. " What should we do ? "

<u>delegates</u>
The leader either identifies the problem or responds to problems raised by the group or one of its members. The problem is given to the group

for them to solve and arrive at a decision. The leader is committed to following their decision and will be available if necessary for consultation. " Will you three sort that out ?"
If the leader is not to be available then the leader can be said to have *abdicated* the leadership role in that situation. The position is as represented by the * asterisk outside the continuum in diagram: 3.
Sometimes a leader may be perceived by the group to have abdicated, in effect by default, as in the case when a leader is unable to give a lead or does not know what to do. If this situation has happened before too often for the group's liking and the leader is unable to or will not delegate to someone else, the situation may deteriorate to the point where it is ripe for the usurpation of power. If this vacuum occurs in a crisis situation it may be filled by a 'contingent' type of leader.
Sharing control is the mark of a more mature leader and is conducive to the development of more effective groups. Put another way, it leads to the development of more effective people in such groups. But leaders do well to remember that the extent to which people may benefit from such methods will also depend on the skills and resources available, the age of the people in the group or their maturity and the length of time the leader and the group have been, or will be, together. Too much responsibility at too early an age in a person's life or too soon in a group's existence, or responsibility for problem solving that is very complex or difficult for present experience and capacities to cope with, can undermine confidence. If the way a group handles its power is not discretely monitored or even at times supervised, the abuse of power by bullies or over-domineering members may destroy belief in the democratic process as a credible way of doing things. Just as importantly, it may also deny the development of other members' potential.

<u>situational leadership</u> - <u>Hersey and Blanchard</u> [7]
This model looks at the leadership situation in terms of orientation options, the orientations being either 'tasks' or 'relationships'.
It posits that a certain sort of situation is best served by a particular

style of leadership.
A leader, trying to discern the appropriate style of leadership to be used in a specific situation must:

a) assess the relative importance of a specific task. i.e. importance might be measured by how difficult or complex the job is: or how vital or soon its completion is to the well being of the group.

b) take into account the quality of the relationships behaviour in the group. i.e. how well they get on together, including their skill level and cooperative capacity and whether or not those relationships would be requisite to the achievement of the task.

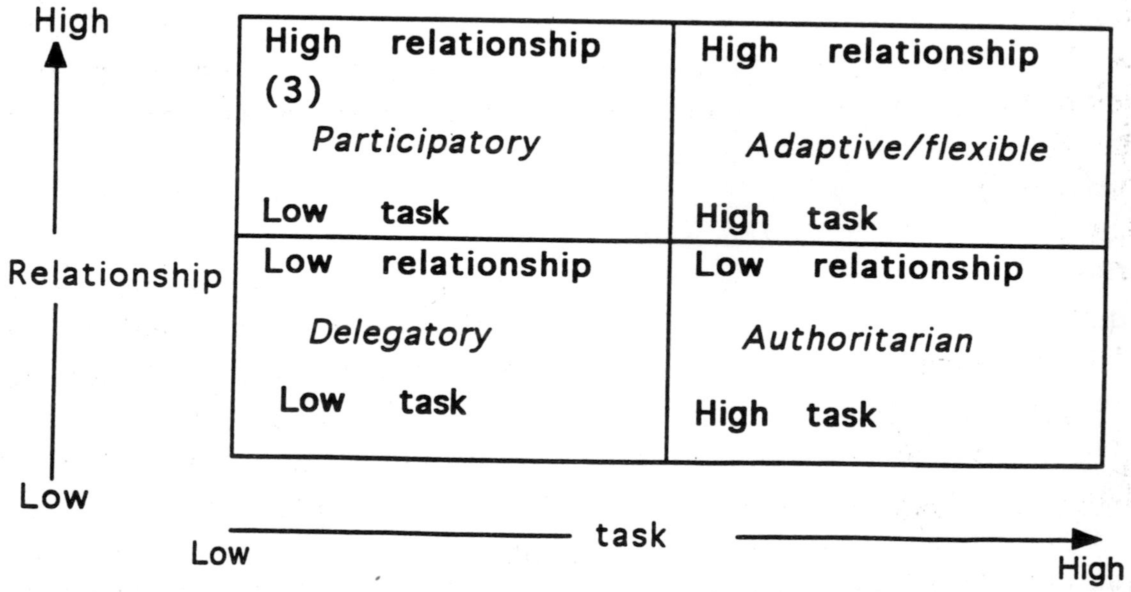

Diagram: 4. Hersey & Blanchard's grid of task/relationship orientations

For example, a leader confronted with the need to improvise an emergency evacuation of an injured member of a party (high task) of fractious novices (low relationships), would be authoritarian because it would be the style most suited to getting the job done quickly. Such a style would be a less appropriate choice for a highly experienced, trained group of friends (high relationships). In the first instance the leader would be authoritarian and directive, whilst in the second case, where both task and relationships are high, it would be more effective to be less directive and take a greater account of the group's skills and resources (more relationship-orientated) by being more flexible and adaptive.

1. high task/low relationships

This category is well illustrated in the early stages of a group's life when the members are uncertain of each other, not too sure about the leader and a bit hazy about the objective. The important thing is to get the task moving by feeding in much information and perhaps imparting a lot of skill. In this situation the leader will be doing a lot of telling and directing and staying in charge. Personal feelings and group needs will be secondary to the achievement of the task. Emergencies would come into this category.

2. high task/high relationships

In this situation the leader will be active and visible but not necessarily directive. A lot is going on, as say in the 'storming' phase of a group's life (see later in this section for 'Tuckman on Groups'). Questions to do with 'why' rather than 'what' are being asked so reasons and explanations are required in order to persuade and convince. Good relationships are as important as getting on with the job because at this juncture, if the relationships become too fouled up, the task falls apart too. The leader's role tends to become political and diplomatic in essence particularly when conflicts, a feature of this phase, have to be resolved positively.

The leader has to be flexible in order to be able to adapt to a variety of conditions or situations. The sustained exercise of a single leadership style here might well be disastrous.

3. <u>low task/high relationships</u>

Here, roles have been assigned to, or assumed by, group members with the skills and ability to undertake them. Control of some things is moving naturally away from the leader. But it is important that, with the removal of this cohesive influence, group harmony is maintained so that the various parts continue to work well together. In order not to become too distant from the group, it is now possible for the leader's focus to move away from the task, and concentrate more on the needs and wants of the group and the individuals in it. The leader will thus participate on a level nearer to the group by joining, sharing, testing and consulting as in the 'norming' phase (see later in this section for 'Tuckman on Groups'). On some expeditions leadership never gets beyond this phase because of the leader's need to feel his/her skills are being fully used: some leaders also like to feel their groups are always dependent upon them. This is a limited view and can be considered as unjust or selfish in that it blocks the development of others.

4. <u>low task/low relationships</u>

In this situation, the leader is concerned to allow his/her role to become low key in order that the group is able to become self functioning to the extent that it, or individuals in it, can see what needs to be done, set up tasks, take most of the decisions, and carry them out. The leader will be mostly delegating, consulting a little, supervising a lot and monitoring all the time. A typical example of this sort of situation would be a group well on the way to self sufficiency as say with an established, fairly well trained and experienced group, preparing to go on a semi-unaccompanied expedition as part of the training for the Duke of Edinburgh Award Scheme. I am aware that there is a possibility of the reader becoming confused here. Within the expedition group there will need to be high relationships in order to carry out a task that may be simple at times and complex at others. So how does this fit into the category of "low task/low relationship?. The distinguishing feature here is that it is the relationship between leader and group that needs to be less involved, looser or 'lower'.

A simpler example would be telling a group to set out chairs for a meeting. The task is simple and consequences not serious if they mismanage it, nor are high degree skills and cooperation required. Also for the purposes of this model it does not matter whether the task is delegated by request or command. Once it is delegated, the involvement of the leader with the group is decreased.

" Control of some things is moving naturally away from the leader"

• The Hersey Blanchard model can be improved by the inclusion of two qualifications.

The response to a situation that is *planned* for may well differ from the response if the same situation is *unplanned* i.e. is confronted unexpectedly. The lack of any opportunity to stage simulations or full rehearsals may mean a group is unprepared both psychologically and in terms of skills. The leader may have the equipment, but the impact of the unexpected will impose a greater burden and probably constrain the leader to be more directive but alert to the need to boost morale and motivation.

Similarly, in the matter of relationship behaviour, a distinction needs to be drawn between the quality of relationships that *is actually present* in a group and the kind of relationship behaviour that *would be required* (and may not be present) to complete a task. If the required level of relationship skill in the group is inadequate for the proposed task, a more directive style may be needed to compensate and provide the means to attain the necessary teamwork for the achievement of the task.

conceptual limitations caused by uniformity of groups and settings

One other important lesson to do with groups is highlighted by the Hersey Blanchard model. In their normal working situations, most practising leaders tend to meet groups that are similar in nature so their thinking and discoveries about leadership will have been constrained within narrower confines. A scout or guide leader will tend to conceptualise leadership in terms of the types of girls and boys s/he customarily leads and will see aims more in terms of independency. The teacher of a remedial group handling youngsters usually less able to fend for themselves will have different ideas about leadership set in his/her mind and will be more inclined to operate with the group in a 'dependency' mode. Unless leaders are normally working with a wide range of different kinds of group, the point might not be realised that ideas about the nature of leadership may be restricted if leaders have only ever worked with one kind of group. If the group is always all boys or all girls or mixed, or if they are usually juniors, adolescents or adults, the nature of the group with which the leader normally works, will colour and to some extent limit a leader's conceptualisation about the nature of leadership. Frequency of meeting can be another limiting factor. How well do you know them? Is it always a "one-off" situation as in an outdoor centre or is it the first time or one of many meetings? Situation sometimes exercises a constraint on outlook too, and therefore practice, if the setting never changes. Can individuals normally seen in the classroom, be expected to exhibit the same characteristics when in the outdoors, or as is quite likely, will the new and different situation throw up surprising traits and reveal unsuspected qualities calling for new and different responses from the leader?

Leaders need to be aware that thinking about how they lead, can be restricted by the uniformity of the group situation they normally experience. When their employment situation changes, as it sometimes does, and different kinds of groups present themselves, ideas about the nature of groups that were previously seen as immutable, are suddenly drastically challenged. Such ideas are more easily modifiable if the leader has been aware that other group situations exist that are different.

conditional theory of leadership - Chase-Priest [8]

Chase and Priest's theory of Conditional Leadership identifies a number of factors which influence when a particular leadership style is used and integrates all these into one model. Leaders' general value orientations [which may be 'people-centred' by virtue of being focussed on maintaining themselves, caring for individual members, building the group relations; or which may be 'things or task-centred' because they are focussed on achieving the task at hand, supporting the sponsoring authority, protecting the natural environment] and the range of leader styles available should flex and change depending on whether a high or low condition exists in five key areas: the favourability of conditions for a particular style is determined by the low/high ratings obtaining in:

1. Degree of environmental danger.
2. Level of individual competence.
3. Degree of group unity.
4. Leader's level of proficiency.
5. Degree of seriousness consequent upon a decision.

The converse of these five factors would clearly imply a decreasing favourability as when the group is divided, leadership is deficient, individuals are incompetent, environmental dangers are many and the consequences of a decision are major.

The degree to which there is a high or low condition in each of these five areas will create circumstances conducive to the adoption of either more directive or less directive styles identified by Chase and Priest as autocratic, democratic and abdicratic (delegatory).

The model is a sophisticated one and considerable effort is required to grasp its essentials sufficiently to be able to apply it in practice.
It is however a model more finely tuned to the needs of the outdoor situation where levels of concern for the care and wellbeing of the individual (services driven) are likely to be higher than in the cut and thrust realms of industry and commerce (market driven - aggressive competition for profit) from which most leadership models originated.

The key point to pick up here is that no one style can be right all the time. The most effective style is one that is flexible to changing situations.

<u>group development</u> - <u>Tuckman</u> [9]

Reference was made earlier to the length of time a group has been, or will be together as a factor bearing on the leadership style to be adopted. A descriptive account of how the life cycle of a group generally develops will be useful at this point. It will be seen that time and timing is an important consideration for leaders.

When a group comes together for whatever reason, there are five identifiable stages it goes through as the group members become better acquainted with the goal or task and each others' strengths and weaknesses. As this knowledge develops so does their effectiveness and the need for leaders to adapt and modify their styles of leading. This scenario should be seen as more relevant to 'teenagers' and onwards than it would be for say, junior children.

1. Forming - the forming phase occurs as group members make initial contact with each other and the leader. It is characterised by a feeling of uncertainty about each other and whether there is some link or purpose common to all present. The life history of the group is coloured by the process of finding out the answers to these queries. There is a higher awareness of the leader as the group seeks information and direction and tries to come to terms with the task and each other. The leader has a fairly high profile at this time.

2. Storming - as the group gains in confidence, and control of decision making begins to shift from the leader to the group, relationships begin to go through a more searching and sometimes an aggressive phase (see below '*'). The transition can result in power conflicts and their resultant pecking orders, but the shift in control is essential if an effectively functioning group is to develop. This is also the shake-down phase which groups need to be helped through fairly quickly, and ideally with as little stress as possible.

* The storming phase can be much influenced by the leadership style adopted, with considerable subsequent repercussions on the norming phase which follows it. The competitive aggression of insecure males (young or old) trying to dominate a mixed group is often allowed to prevail in the struggle for power and pecking orders because that is

how the leader (male) operates naturally. Many able, perhaps less assertive but probably more effective people, will become alienated and thus uninvolved in the group because they feel they can have no say or power unless they are prepared to descend to the jungle-like behaviour of the dominators. The leader has to make it quite clear that the "survival of the fittest" ethic is not at all acceptable and that there are other more productive alternatives to the 'dog eat dog' way of being.

3. Norming - hopefully the result of the storming phase is that the group members manage to get on with each other sufficiently well to function effectively. Roles become apparent or are defined, strengths and weaknesses are recognised, compromises are negotiated. The group has arrived at an agreed shared goal and an acceptable culture to live by. A norm is a rule, either implicit or explicit, that says what behaviour is acceptable in that group, e.g. a speaker should not be interrupted.

4. Performing - all the group's energy is directed to achieving the goal. Everyone is playing a full part and problems are tackled openly. This phase is often described as *synergetic* , i.e. the sum of the whole is greater than the sum of the parts. Morale and achievement are high.

5. Adjourning - this is the winding down phase prior to the disbanding of the group. There may be sadness at the imminence of parting but the focus will be on tying up loose ends, reminiscing and evaluating. The leader can harness this climate for more formally directed reflection and reviewing aimed at drawing out the lessons to be learned from the experience that would otherwise never surface to conscious awareness. People like tidy endings to their experiences and a few concluding words from the leader is the sort of informal ceremony that fits the bill nicely.

Knowledge of this developmental group process is useful to leaders in

giving them some idea of what to expect. They are able to view as relatively normal for example, the more alarming aspects of the storming phase. They are not prevented, by a defensive reaction, from monitoring the group's progress closely in order that their style of leadership is in accord with the current stage of progress.
It is as well to be aware however, that this model, in outlining the various stages a group can go through, can convey the erroneous impression that movement in a group is always forward. Group development can regress and appear to deteriorate periodically, displaying what is best described as the 'peaks and troughs' phenomenon. Things do not always occur in the theoretical order expected.

This model, whilst very useful, only touches the tip of the iceberg. There is much more that leaders need to know about groups. For example, the different positive and negative roles that people can take on in groups which help or hinder the performance of a task or when engaged in building up the group itself.(for more detail see Tables: 2-5 at the end of this section and 'people/task behaviours' in section 5) The role of peer group influences, past and present, is also significant knowledge for the understanding of the life of groups.

style stereotypes

Before leaving the subject, there are other important implications embedded in leadership styles that should be considered. They are best studied by looking at some polarised examples of leadership which will highlight the important differences for both the leader and members of the group.

the coercive or leader-centred style

The average person in the street asked for their idea of a leader will usually give the military model. The leader is conceived to be all important, so is very authoritarian. There is a very clear hierarchy of leader and follower. The required behaviour of such a group is conformity and obedience to all orders. Independent thought is not normally encouraged or required. This style may be very good for the battle field, parade ground or emergency situations where both time and need require rapid and immediate action. But applied to other types of situations or tasks it may be quite inappropriate. It can cramp initiative, dampen enjoyment, reduce the feeling of being involved and even hinder the development of those relationships essential for getting the job done. In the military situation it works because the 'team' realises in battle that survival may depend on unquestioning obedience, whilst off the battlefield there are the well known penalties that can be enforced for disobedience. Leaders are perceived to be vested with a considerable power to punish.

Leaders preferring this style tend to believe that there is a best way to teach a particular body of knowledge, and by implication, only one way to learn it. They spend a lot of time working out this best way and perfecting and updating it. Knowledge is presented comprehensively in as neat and logical an order as possible. Demonstrations have to be as near perfect as possible. Mistakes are perceived as time wasting and to be avoided. This style leads by presenting models of perfection to the group and the learning style is characterised by rote-learning, imitating or copying. Such leaders also tend to be very achievement orientated and therefore set great store by efficiency, careful planning and preparation. They will be very methodical, in order to avoid untidy loose ends and time wasting. Their treatment of their subject will be very detailed and comprehensive. The framework within which they work will tend to be rigid and not easily able to flex for the unexpected, or adapt to people of varying abilities and motivation. Such leaders often hold perfectionist values.

Out-of-doors this style can be identified as the kind of leadership that leads by example - a force pulling the group along from the front. Unless care is taken the tail end may suffer. If leaders of this type are highly skilled and competent they may be so far removed from the level of skill in a party that they are unaware of, or unsympathetic to, any difficulties that individuals in the group may be experiencing. Being at the front, they will tend to take all the decisions all the time. The group will not be involved in the experience as much as it might be and will tend to be tagging along blindly. It will have no real idea of what is happening or of the whys, wheres and hows of it all. No one will have any sense of ownership in the enterprise.

" Leaders are perceived to be vested with a considerable power to punish "

<u>the permissive or person-centred style</u>

Here the leadership style is fairly low profile in order to encourage the people in the group to express themselves and take initiatives. The style may even seem to be, though it is not, "laissez-faire" in character, which is a complete absence of leadership. Power is devolved to the group in order to create the space for learning of a special kind, called experiential learning, which is based on being involved in real experiences. It is accepted that some things in life cannot be taught. It is recognised that it is necessary, and only possible, for people to learn certain kinds of lesson by being left alone to get on with it and discover for themselves. Being allowed to be responsible for one's own learning means experiencing one's own mistakes and successes in real situations. There is a well known definition of an expert as one who has made the most mistakes so knows the subject inside out. This method may be somewhat time-consuming, untidy and at times seemingly anarchic. But it can flex to the unexpected and be spontaneous. It is also individualistic or to use the jargon, client-centred. If the level of self motivation of members of the group is not carefully monitored by the leader however, inter-personal competitiveness may arise to the extent that wholesome assertiveness may deteriorate into an undesirable aggressiveness which will block productive expression and initiative.

Leaders used to more authoritarian ways of working, may be unsure about how much freedom can be given to a group and have real worries about the apparent lack of the 'normal' controls and things running away on them. Controls exist in all styles but they vary in kind, so the problem is a question of identifying them. One way of finding out is to discuss thoroughly the freedom/authority issue and what it means and implies with the group. Agreement can be reached by negotiation or by the leader setting limits. Such limits would normally include the four basic provisos that whatever is decided must not be illegal, unsafe, or harmful either emotionally or physically, to any member in the group. Neither can such decisions be binding upon anyone outside the group.

This may seem to be obvious, but it can be forgotten in emotionally charged situations.

This type of leadership would tend to be found at the rear of the group - a force pushing the group from the back. This does not mean, as it sometimes happens, that the leader goes to the back but continues to tell the group what to do from there. To be physically at the rear whilst continuing to project a directive lead is to display all the characteristics of the front placed leader.

Leading from the rear is a figurative attitude, but may be literally a physical position. The concern here may be to allow those at the front to feel they are involved and exercising some initiative in the shape of the day. There is also present a humane concern to encourage the weaker ones who tend to be in the rear. The danger here is the leader's loss of control at the front unless some thought has been given to the problem. First hand knowledge of the ground is needed so that a leader can anticipate when there may be a need to return to the front to cope with any tricky sections of the journey. The leader needs to know the party well enough to be able to rely on them not moving beyond the contact range of eye, ear or voice, as necessary to the situation. Recognisable points can be set at which the front should halt to allow the rear to catch up. A more experienced group may be content to go at the pace of the slowest, but techniques need devising to cope with the impulsiveness of novice groups. The skill is to maintain enthusiasm and enjoyment without losing control. To regard this role as one of maintaining control without killing enthusiasm is a negative way of approaching the situation.

<u>the consultative/participative or group-centred style</u>

This style tends to work either by consensus or in a formal democratic manner. It requires a group to be confident and skillful enough to cooperate and participate, particularly in the process of communication and information exchanging so that opinions may be offered, worries are aired, problems solved, decisions made, and goals achieved. This style depends as much on the group for success as on the designated leader. In this it differs from the other two styles. When decisions about ends, aims or content are required, they are determined by the whole group. Where preferences about means are sought, (pace, speed, standard, pitch, degree etc.) they will be self regulated by the group. This style is underpinned by the belief that if the relationships in the group are right, anything is possible. The style also has the in-built flexibility to operate periodically under either of the other two styles if the group chooses to do so.

A morning meeting that was making decisions about the programme for the day was disrupted by the intrusion of events in the recent history of the group. Earlier on, a lot of resentment had arisen around the table tennis table about whose turn it should be to play next. A lively exchange was now allowed to take place which became a matter of fierce argument about whether the winner of the previous game always earned the right to be one of the players in the next game or whether it should be a completely different pair. An important issue for them about fairness and justice was at stake. If left unresolved it would have serious effects on the harmony and cohesion of the group and the achievement of their aims. The priorities of an authoritarian regime concerned about getting on with activities (task) might have swept the whole thing under the carpet as an irrelevant side issue - with untold consequences. The democratic mode of operation required the leader to admit a different set of priorities which was prepared to put achievement in activities 'on hold'. It was felt important to give time to an exploration of the true nature of fairness which was for the first time ever for some of them and was instrumental in helping mistaken beliefs to be corrected. If this episode is read as putting table-tennis before more important matters, the whole point has been missed.

On the move in the field, a leader using this style tends to be found in the middle of the group - a position which epitomises the modern dynamic concept of leadership. Such a leadership style will be a combination of all of the styles mentioned above. The leader will only be authoritarian or military in style sparingly, at those times when occasion or situation demand it- perhaps only in emergencies or when physical safety is threatened by ignorance or fool-hardiness in the group. Using this consultative style, the leader can be at the front, centre or back according to the indications picked up from the physical environment and the group. The style tends to work democratically, helping, but not generally dictating to, the group to resolve their different impulses and inclinations, to decide for themselves, to adopt and carry through their plans. The leader is watchful to give support, encouragement, sympathy, guidance or advice to those individuals who need help. Leaders should be tuned in to signs of discomfort, stress or anxiety and be alive to possibilities that will arouse interest in and enthusiasm for, the natural environment. The leader is at once consultant, counsellor, guide, mentor, chaperone and a source of information, knowledge, skill and experience. The leader is less a leader and more a person whose experience and resources are at the service of the group. The group is helped to lead itself as far as it is judged capable of doing so.

a comparative note on style

The directive style tends to accentuate teaching behaviour. There is often an implicit belief that learning can only take place after teaching, i.e. teaching is essential to learning. There is a place for this and it is true in some respects, but not for everything. Under this regime there tends to be a quicker and maybe a more systematic coverage of material - which can be mistaken for efficiency. But the criterion for efficiency is surely whether the thing that is taught is absorbed, learned and understood. However, much depends on what is meant by the term 'learning'. Directed learning tends to be at second hand, somewhat mechanical and imitative, rote learning for example, so understanding is not always as thorough as it should be. With experience-based methods, as found in permissive or democratic styles, the emphasis is on learning behaviour by discovery and experience. Self motivated participation is required. Experience-based learning by definition is first hand and real. Because it has been experienced in a real life situation, it is experienced by all of the capacities of a person working together simultaneously so it is integrated and holistic - unlike the directive, didactic approach which tends to reduce material into its various separate parts in order to understand each in isolation (reductionist). But as with directed learning, experience may not be fully appreciated unless supported by a reflective, reviewing process.

Leaders should know that the same group of people will behave in markedly different ways under different styles; e.g. aggression and hostility is more frequent with autocratic and laissez faire styles. There tends to be more scape-goating in an autocratic regime too. Member satisfaction is associated with the democratic style and is highest in small interaction-oriented groups. As always, different styles are effective under different conditions.

<u>a note on the democratic process</u>

It is sometimes difficult for leaders to know how actually to begin operating in the democratic mode. Is it done in a formal way by an announcement to that effect which may have a group of young people wondering what this new stunt is and begin testing out with outrageous suggestions to see what happens. If it is done informally and naturally in the course of events, it may be even more difficult for the group to discern when the offer of sharing power is being made. On the other hand, the transition from one style to another can be easily natural because the situation obviously requires it and the nature of prevailing relationships causes no problems. How this style is introduced to a particular group may need some thinking about. It is sometimes necessary to spend some time on this in order to make clear what the implications for the group are in terms of their responses and behaviour. Especially if it is unfamiliar, they may need to understand in order that ground rules for operating this way can be established; even to the extent of reminding them how a proper discussion is carried out since the orderly exchange of ideas is crucial to the success of this style. Whether a lot is left to a process of discovery or not, at some time there will need to develop an understanding that the method depends on a number of things for success:

• Two-way communication must happen or the method will wither.

• Nothing will happen unless the group exert themselves to make it happen. Even then it may not happen in the way that was expected or hoped since events sometimes have a disturbing habit of taking over or intervening. Unequal patterns of individual participation too can create a breakdown of relationships. If some appear to be doing or saying nothing, the inactivity or silence may be misinterpreted to arouse strong feelings about unfairness.

• Trust amongst the members is essential to make agreements about rules, or whatever, stick.

• Sincerity and consistency in the leader is vital. Cynical, worldly-wise attitudes of these times tend to see things like promises and agreements as so much naive optimism. Group discussions in reaching informal understandings or formal contracts about behaviour, can spell out the consequences of breaking promises or agreements and re-invest these social conventions with their need to be taken seriously.

There may be problems in introducing the democratic style with school groups such as:

• the testing out of staff by pupils to find out where the limits are in this new situation.

• the suspicions of staff in other departments need to be allayed by careful preparation of the ground with them beforehand.

- old habits acquired in response to the tight scheduling of normal time-tabling will be found to contravene the requirements of the democratic process, e.g. the Staff says, 'hurry up and answer, we haven't much time', the Student says, 'no wait, I need more time and space to think about or respond to questions that are quite different from those I usually get asked'.

Democratic leaders need to be stable, secure people able to take the risks of treading a knife edge. In our society, leaders will be held responsible for the actions of those in their charge even when the leader's power has been delegated. It is a different kind of risk taking and must be backed by a strong belief in the rightness of the cause and by convictions that can be articulated to whomsoever sees fit to take you to task " for being irresponsible in letting them have their own way"-which is how Mr. or Mrs. Average Citizen regrettably tend to view it. At times leaders will be aware that they are close to flying in the face of normal conventions. If things go wrong the leader will be seen to be answerable. I remember once being reprimanded by an irate member of the public who was outraged at the misdoings, in an unsupervised moment, of some of the young people for whom I was responsible. A philosophic discussion about the nature of man and self responsibility would not have been well received at the time and in a moment of inspiration all I could respond with was a promise that if the time came when the police would be held responsible for the wrong doings of the criminal fraternity, then I would be prepared to be responsible for the actions of my group. Whilst that floored him for the moment it did not exactly solve the problem. Mulling it over later, I reached the conclusion that if someone in a group decides to go off the rails, there is not a lot you can usually do about it at the time. The leader cannot really be held responsible for the anti-social decisions or actions of others. The only way to guarantee such things did not happen would be to chain them to their beds! Ships are built for leaving harbour we are told and the same applies to people, otherwise what is the point of their existence? Later what a leader can do, is be responsible for picking up the pieces, ensuring that damage of whatever kind is made good by the perpetrators and going over the episode with the miscreants in an attempt to get them to see the error of their ways or reach a tighter contract-type agreement with them.

" At times leaders will be aware that they are close to flying............."

style pitfalls

In adopting leadership styles, leaders need to be aware that after aims have been formulated, it is possible to choose a style which, if used as a general strategy rather than as an occasional, expedient tactic, may either help or hinder the aims. It is sometimes not appreciated that it is possible to match up aims with a style of leadership which will ensure that the aims are never achieved ! For example, if the aim was to help the group become more self-determining and self-sufficient, as would be the case in preparing a group to undertake an unaccompanied expedition in the Duke of Edinburgh Award Scheme, the coercive style in requiring mindless dependence and initiative-stripping conformity, would be quite incongruent. It would be appropriate for an emergency situation where an authoritarian style is the best choice and may help to impart confidence in the group and get things done quickly.

Canoe novices might be better left to learn by discovery the intricacies of paddling in a straight line, whilst reserving more directive coaching for the slower learner or the more complex strokes that may come later in the same session.

The autocratic style would be unsuitable to the teacher who wished the group to experience a more relaxed and informal environment in order to develop a better relationship with, and between them.

A group struggling with the complexities of navigation might be served better by a 'permissive' unaccompanied simple journey along the valley bottoms than by a coerced, complex, guided marathon over the tops.

A tent pitching session can be turned from a boringly didactic ordeal into an hilarious, heuristic exercise of the intellect by choosing to use the permissive style.

It is important to make clear if the point has not already been emphasised, that when a particular style is chosen, it does not have to be for the whole of a skills training session or for all of a more extended programme but only for bits of it. To take the example about a Duke of Edinburgh Award expedition above, it may still be necessary to use a directive style on occasion to achieve a short term objective although the long term aim is independence and self-sufficiency. A particular style might only be used for five minutes, or it may be required for three hours, or three days because it is the appropriate tactic for the aim, the group, the individual or the occasion !

<u>limitations and possibilities of situations in activities</u>

Different outdoor activities are characterised by situations that impose their own particular limitations on the choice of leadership style. It is likely to be more difficult to give close support or coaching to individuals in their own vessels when canoeing or sailing, or in a restricted passage in caving, or on the open hillside when skiing, than it is, for example, to a group on a mountain walk, by the very nature of the way the activity is performed. In some situations only one style is appropriate. What do you do in a cave where most of the group are out of sight for much of the time?

"What do you do in a cave where most of the group are out of sight?

Whilst most of the novice-learner type situations require a fair degree of directive control, there are more opportunities for discovery methods than one might at first think. But where mistakes by a group member would have very serious consequences, supervision would have to be tight. In light winds, an unaccompanied dinghy crew could be allowed to learn by experience in a way that would be unthinkable in very strong winds where a very authoritarian style from an instructor on board would be more appropriate. Also the sheer proximity of instructor and crew at close quarters in a dinghy makes it less easy to give the crew space to think independently. Even small detail is too easily directed, so the crew tend to stop thinking. Competitive racing is different obviously-but the habit of heavy command can overlap into recreative sailing.

The command structure in the less crowded situation of keel boats, is an interesting phenomenon especially when sailing in navigable waters. Boat skippers are like car drivers in that they have legal responsibilities to avoid collision. This makes the activity an exception to some extent because it is circumscribed by legislation in a way that does not yet apply to the other activities in the U.K., though it applies to them now on the Continent. (But if EEC regulations relating to the suppliers of services become law in the U.K., anyone charged with negligence will be assumed guilty until proved innocent.) Training skippers have a difficult task in trying to discern how far to be directive and how far to delegate. If the crew becomes too used to democratic methods, will the habits encouraged by this style, such as expecting a say in the shaping of events, inadvertently arise during emergencies to endanger the ship or others in the vicinity? Skippers may tend to be directive on a boat because they are responsible and accountable in law for a wide range of liabilities. They may try to delegate but may feel obliged to keep intervening in a way that will affect initiative and the means to foster self sufficiency.

Rock climbing can be an activity that is very flexible in providing situations that readily permit different leadership styles. This is illustrated by looking at the ways a person can be coached up a route. A directive style would point out every hold and instruct how every move should be made. No thought would be required of the learner, just acquiescence. With a permissive style no instruction would be given at all. But a safety structure would be provided by the rope and novices would be allowed to work everything out for themselves. A laissez-faire style would provide more experienced students with a technical manual and guide book and, having delegated all responsibility to them absolutely, leave them to get on with it completely by themselves. A democratic style would allow everyone to be involved in and responsible for belaying and taking in the rope or securing and paying out the rope to another student. Shades of difference in between these styles would be seen in the leader operating a diagnostic and reflective approach (as with a mirror) which by summarising and identifying the situation, thereby facilitates the resolution of the problem for the student, thus: " You are not in balance, you need to find something for your right foot". Or, " If you do not move soon, your arms will tire and you will fall off. Climb down to a comfortable stance and think again." On occasion none of these methods will work and it will become necessary to persuade and encourage the disheartened follower, " You're O.K. I've got you on the rope. You can do it. Have a rest first, then try again."

tables - highlighting differences between styles

An aspirant leader grappling with the novel intricacies of leading styles does not always immediately appreciate the important distinctions that must be drawn. It takes time to understand just what differences are entailed by a variation in style and what this means in terms of the kinds of behaviour that both the leader and the members of a group must adopt and in terms of the sorts of skills they must have. In an attempt to assist this process, a number of tables[10] follow which try to tease out and show some of these differences.

TABLE. 1.

Table 1. can be read across the page so that a characteristic in one style column has its corresponding characteristic in the other two style columns.

THE DIFFERENT CHARACTERISTICS OF THREE TYPES OF LEADERSHIP STYLE

COERCIVE STYLE	PERMISSIVE STYLE	CONSULTATIVE STYLE
Leader directed.	**Individual** self directed.	**Group** acts collectively.
Authoritarian control.	Delegatory but not laissez-faire, which is non-control or abdication.	Consensus control by group.
Imposed aims/tasks.	Self selected aims/tasks.	Group determined aims/tasks
Hierarchical structure necessary.	Anarchical structure can result.	Democratic/representative structure develops.
Conformity required.	Initiative & self-expression required. May become competitive.	Cooperation and trust required. Can include other styles if wished.
Rigid framework-rules etc. imposed.	Relaxed framework.	Flexible, adaptive framework. Rules agreed.
Activity highly organised well planned, methodical. May require much admin. to ensure it works.	Activity is self motivated or opportunist and spontaneous. It may be erratic and random.	Activity develops organically from needs expressed in the group.
Learn from 'models' and applying theory.	Learn by discovery and from experience.	The necessary process of consulting and negotiating is an extra learning experience.
Perfectionist and tidy.	Mistake prone and untidy	Mixture of other two styles.

COERCIVE STYLE	PERMISSIVE STYLE	CONSULTATIVE STYLE
Success/achievement oriented. Getting there is all important.	Failure is possible and accepted.	Mixture of other two styles and often self-correcting. The journey may be more important than getting there.
Mistakes frowned upon or punished.	Mistakes may be demoral--ising	Mistakes are learned from.
Time saving.	Time consuming, not time wasting	Mixture of the other two styles.
Uniform end product or effect on individual is visualised by leader.	End product is individually variable.	Conception about end product is built up by all.
Assumptions made by leader in selection of content/task etc.	Content/task self selected.	Content/task decided by the group.
Content,delivery,speed determined/imposed by leader.	Self regulatory / self imposed.	Self regulatory / self imposed.
Concern is for standards of achievement and results.	Concern is for personal effectiveness.	Concern is for inter-personal relationships and social awareness.
The main focus is upon achieving the task/aim or learning about the subject matter in hand. The style is thus task-oriented or product-oriented.	The main focus is upon personal interests and the style is thus interest oriented. But elements of other styles are often interlaced with it.	The main focus is on the value derived from the group process in terms of social adequacy. The style is thus process-oriented and needs-oriented.

TABLE.2.

LEADERS REQUIRE DIFFERENT ROLES/BEHAVIOURS FOR DIFFERENT STYLES

COERCIVE STYLE	PERMISSIVE STYLE	CONSULTATIVE STYLE
Director	Observer	Observer
Supervisor	Recorder	Recorder
Instructor	Provider(resources)	Facilitator
Leader	Stimulator(ideas)	Commentator
Demonstrator	Opportunist	Helper
Pedagogue	Evaluator	Supporter
Organiser	Coordinator	Mediator
Planner		Consultant
Initiator		Advisor
Disciplinarian		Reflector
Motivator		Delegator
Selector		Evaluator
Judge		Reviewer
Assessor		
Challenger		
Analyser		
Criticiser		

TABLE.3.

LEADERS REQUIRE DIFFERENT SKILLS FOR DIFFERENT STYLES

COERCIVE STYLE	PERMISSIVE STYLE	CONSULTATIVE STYLE
Decision-making	Observing	Responding
Order-giving	Recording	Adapting
Controlling	Approving	Commenting
Dominating	Encouraging	Summarising
Asserting	Keeping low profile	Clarifying
Problem-solving	Suggesting	Identifying questions
Analysing	Supporting	Identifying problems
Confronting	Keeping silent	Identifying decisions
Setting limits	Providing resources	Compensating

COERCIVE STYLE	PERMISSIVE STYLE	CONSULTATIVE STYLE
Giving information	Providing back-up organisation.	Balancing
Giving answers	Monitoring	Reinforcing
Summarising		Supporting
Pace-making		Persuading
Measuring		Giving information
Assessing		Providing resources
Imparting confidence		Catalysing
Taking responsibility		With-holding
Setting aims/tasks		Keeping silent
Criticising		Being patient
Censuring		Confronting
Scolding		Expressing
Disapproving		Interpreting
Approving		Observing
Praising		Recording
		Feeding back
		Evaluating
		Monitoring

TABLE.4.

GROUP MEMBERS REQUIRE DIFFERENT ROLES/BEHAVIOURS FOR DIFFERENT STYLES

COERCIVE STYLE	PERMISSIVE STYLE	CONSULTATIVE STYLE
Conformer	Initiator	Collaborator
Obeyer	Forager	Participator
Follower	Discoverer	Sharer
Receiver	Explorer	Initiator
Absorber	Researcher	Recorder
Imitator	Pace maker	Organiser
Repeater	Selector	Planner
Performer	Decision-maker	Voter
Agreer		Communicator
Complier		

TABLE.5.

GROUP MEMBERS REQUIRE DIFFERENT SKILLS FOR DIFFERENT STYLES *

COERCIVE STYLE	PERMISSIVE STYLE	CONSULTATIVE STYLE
Listening	Inducing	Solving problems
Memorising	Deducing	Making decisions
Reiterating	Relating facts	Carrying out plans
Concentrating	Drawing conclusions	Expressing
Watching	Organising self	Articulating
Copying	Assessing self	Communicating
Collating	Expressing self	Listening
Imitating	Defending self	Responding
	Asserting self	Suggesting
	making decisions	Opining
	making judgments	Feeding back
	Taking initiatives	Judging
	Taking responsibility	Relating
		Cooperating
		Evaluating
		Negotiating
		Taking responsibility

personality and natural leading style

One final point on leadership styles. The way you were brought up, the experiences you have had and the nature of your personality will have tended to impart a set of values and attitudes which will cause a gravitation towards one of the three polarised styles mentioned above. In other words, the way you are and how you are, will determine the style you tend naturally to *prefer* to use. Without training or conscious effort, you are likely to adhere to that style and remain unaware of other styles, or when and how they are best used.

It is important to leading ability that leaders develop a conscious structure of concepts (a model) on which to base their own ideas about leadership. Without such a personal model, it is very difficult to form, develop, or manipulate ideas about a very intangible subject. But once it is acquired, do not forget to spring clean it occasionally !

To summarise this section it can be stated that the choice of leading style may be affected by aims or task, situation or circumstances, the nature of the group and its stage of development (maturity). It is important for the leader to remember that circumstances of situation and needs of group are continually changing. The ability to perceive and evaluate these changes and the possession of a range of styles to be versatile in matching these changes appropriately, are key leadership skills. Research indicates that leadership characteristics and situational demands seem to interact to determine the extent to which a leader will be successful in a group. Previously successful leaders may fail when placed in a situation that demands responses that are incompatible with the leader's personality, or his/her normal pattern of interaction or performance. Training helps to reduce this possibility.

SECTION FIVE

LEADER AWARENESS

comparison of formal and informal party situations

Leading a formal group in the outdoors is a very different 'game' from the informal situation of "being with friends". With friends of equal ability, responsibility and decision-making is shared in a casual almost carefree way. Each is tacitly understood to be self responsible (and for an informal group of adults this is the legal interpretation too) each having the skill and experience to know and observe personal limitations. If one of them has a problem it is assumed that it will be brought to the notice of the others. It would be less easy to do this in a group that often displayed 'one-upmanship' and aggressive competitiveness . Such groups are potential disasters looking for somewhere to happen !

Once the business of leading a formal party is embarked upon, a different world is entered with a new, extra, second dimension containing an additional set of factors to become aware of and to take into account. These factors are mostly to do with managing people and maintaining good working relationships. There is a large element of consideration for others involving self discipline and self denial in party leading which must have been thought through and accepted. It is well known that it is difficult for a leader to control others if self control is lacking. The basis of self control is self awareness and self knowledge.

<u>self awareness</u>

Shifts in personal attitudes and predispositions, changes in preoccupations and priorities, changes in a general attitude to others, occur as a result of a raised level of awareness of self. By way of illustration take the case of a group with a leader not quite sure of his/her whereabouts in mist. It is important this leader <u>be aware</u> that there may be present an anxiety not to lose the way and a need for immediate reassurance that the present position is correctly identified and that a suitable line or track is being followed. These worries could cause the leader gradually to speed up the pace and eventually cause distress to the group. In <u>an unaware state</u> it is a propensity of the emotional condition that the leader is more likely to fall into this acceleration trap.

This kind of awareness could take years to acquire but a few well chosen words during training would achieve the desired effect in moments. The leader would then be aware that if acceleration is undesirable it can be avoided. Alternatively, if acceleration becomes necessary, the change of pace will be conscious and deliberate. There will be a *conscious awareness* that some of the group may be affected. Thus this small piece of awareness will have contributed to that quality of alertness and sensitivity one hopes to see in leaders. This is a typical example of how a piece of theoretical and apparently esoteric knowledge can have a practical use and application.

•Self awareness has other applications which are slightly different, for example, as when trying to put meaning to some puzzling behaviour in a group. (see also sub-section seven on 'observation/perception/ interpretation')

The conclusions a leader draws about human behaviour when it is observed are interpretations of perceptions. Not only is perception selective in tending to see what it wants to see, but the tendency is to judge others by the condition of oneself. This is particularly so when

trying to identify motives in others. Sometimes there is no other helpful information to assist except what can be found from within the personal experience of the leader. The open, trusting sort of leader will find it easier to trust others. Positive motives will be ascribed to the actions of others or at least good and acceptable reasons will be assumed even if they are as yet unknown. An insecure defensive person will tend to suspect the worst in people because threats or insults to self are always looked for. In looking, those negative motives will be found even when they are not there or not intended.
It is important for leaders to be self aware so that personal prejudices can be prevented, as much as is humanly possible, from muddying the waters when interpreting the behaviour of others. Stereo- typing people is a form of prejudice for example. Are leaders aware of it in themselves?

life style states

There are three main orientations with regard to states of self and life styles. [11] One of these tends to be predominant in most people. Leaders should be aware which one obtains personally.

- **'Doing'** kinds of people tend to act first and think later; they 'do' practical things. e.g. explorers, hunters, engineers, builders.

- **'Being'** people by contrast rarely act and are preoccupied with thinking about the state of how they are. e.g. monks, mystics, hippies.

- **'Becoming'** people tend to be a mixture of the other two states. Thinking is used to guide their actions. e.g. you and I !! (Because I am writing this book about becoming and you are reading it)

Leaders who are 'doing' people setting greater store on more tangible, practical types of knowledge, will be less easily convinced about the value of information that falls into the "awareness and understanding" categories. 'Becoming' people operating from a more balanced perspective will feel it to be relatively easy. Identifying which orientation fits personally, places a leader in a better position to see whether one of the other orientations is better suited to leadership and towards which personal movement is required.

practical points for personal awareness

It is important that the following points about the leading situation are realised:

- Although there will be a group present, it is virtually a 'solo' situation for the leader in the sense that there may be no other person with whom, in extremity, the responsibility of decision-making and navigating can be shared -unless of course the leader is fortunate enough to have a second experienced person along as a designated assistant. The group may be encouraged to participate in these activities, but still the onus will be on the leader to check they are correct or acceptable. The leader is the one held accountable.

- The whole group is dependent on the leader to the extent that, in the final analysis, s/he is responsible for their enjoyment, comfort and safety.

- You may have to do all the thinking for each and everyone of them - especially if they are novices to the extent even of telling them, for example, when to eat, drink, put on extra clothing/waterproofs or take them off, tie up boot laces or adjust rucksack straps.

- You may not assume that what you can do, they can also do.

- You may not even assume that what you want to do within the day will coincide with their desires and aspirations. This is one aspect served well by the democratic style of leadership which keeps channels of communication open and gives you vital feedback on how the group reads the situation.

awareness of the group's condition-signs and signals

Leaders should not assume that because they personally feel comfortable, relaxed, confident, at any given moment, the members of the group feel the same. For all that can be known, members of the group may quite likely be too hot, too cold, thirsty, hungry, out of breath, miserable, over-awed, anxious, tense, bored, fed-up or plain tired. Watch for 'signals' being displayed.

" Leaders should not assume that because they feel comfortable, relaxed and confident..................members of the group feel the same."

An in-depth knowledge about the nature of verbal and non verbal communication is very useful. For all manner of reasons, people do not always mean what they say. A boy's response to a concerned query which draws a, " Whose afraid? Not me! " may be blustered out in such a way as to mean the opposite. But signals may not always be verbal. There are vocal clues in the pitch, speed, volume, inflection, tone and emphasis of the voice - grunts, groans, sighs, various noises and worst of all to interpret, silence. It is the non verbal modes of communication which give a more subtle but reliable feedback. Very revealing indications come from facial expressions, gestures, attitudes of body posture, restlessness, gait and other mannerisms. Harder to detect are some of the involuntary signals the body gives out - rapid breathing or pulse rate, dryness in the mouth, pupil dilation, fear induced sweating. Does that yawn mean fear, tiredness or boredom? Is that redness caused by sheer physical exertion, blushing or flushing? Is that white pallor a symptom of imminent sickness, caused by pain or fear or is it a low body temperature? Anxiety, physical distress, feelings of inadequacy, dangerous levels of exhilaration or exuberance (as when high quality environments are experienced) which could lead to life endangering foolishness or recklessness, all need to be watched out for and monitored in case your intervention is required. Be aware of the group. Awareness is one of the foundation stones of control. Desmond Morris gives further insights into this fascinating topic in his book 'Manwatching' [12].

awareness of group behaviour

Benefits accrue from an awareness of peoples' needs [5] and how they behave when they are in groups. As individuals in a one-to-one exchange with you, they can be quite pleasant people. In groups, the pressure of not losing face, keeping one's end up, establishing status in the group, being egged on to do things or "You won't be one of us" (and remember that they do want to belong to the peer group), being put down, being shown up, embarrassed, belittled and so forth are all very powerful triggers that can cause people to behave quite out of character. Books[13] have been written which identify many of the so-called "behaviour games" people play, often unconsciously, in their transactions with each other. A knowledge of some of the games is a useful aid to the understanding and interpretation of some of the behavioural aspects of group life. Knowing whether to tackle or ignore something seen depends on how significant it is in relation to other things. This can be a minefield. To do something about 'games' is quite difficult because the behaviour pattern is likely to be quite deeply entrenched and often the product of home and neighbourhood experiences. Sometimes just being able to identify the game and cause a group to become aware of what is going on can be enough to stop it. Common games are:- '*uproar* ' (which is when a person uses some minor irritation to 'erupt' at authority in a way out of all proportion to the cause in order to attract status) or '*smoke screens* ' (when a group seems to orchestrate a number of minor incidents in order to distract authority from dealing with the misdemeanour that started it all off) or '*how far can we push him before he loses his temper*' or '*if we keep silent long enough "Sir/Miss" will give us the answer*'.

people/task behaviour in groups

Groups or leaders when working towards some aim, tend to be in one of two modes. These are:

- Getting on with the aim, goal or task.
- Maintaining or mending relationships.

Roles in such groups often reflect these two modes. Leaders may find them a useful tool to understand or diagnose who is doing what in the group. Some of these roles were itemised in the tables at the end of section four, but can be looked at in another useful way from the point of view of these two modes. Any member of the group may show leadership behaviour by taking action that helps the group achieve the task or maintain effective relationships.
Thus we have:

Task actions which are leadership actions.

Information and opinion giver
Information and opinion seeker
Direction and role definer
Summariser
Energiser
Comprehension checker

Maintenance actions which are leadership actions.

Encourager of participation
Communication facilitator
Tension reliever
Process observer
Interpersonal problem solver
Supporter and praiser

dominance/sociability behaviour in groups

When two or more people interact, the nature of that interpersonal behaviour may be described in ways which seem to be the same as the above since they are to do with authority and control or friendliness and intimacy. They are closely related in a way, but they are also distinct. For example most people like either to control things (high dominance) or let others do the controlling (low dominance). We can be in one mode or the other at different times for various reasons. Also, most people tend to be warm and personal (high sociability) or to be cool and impersonal (low sociability). Again either is possible depending on circumstances. These four variables can be broken down into more significant classifications[14] as shown in diagram 5.
These may help when it is necessary for a leader to know what is happening between and among individuals in the group and know whether to do anything about it in a way that will be positive and avoid unproductive outcomes. Interpreting human behaviour is a difficult skill. The ability to do it fairly reliably and consistently is a tremendous asset to a leader.

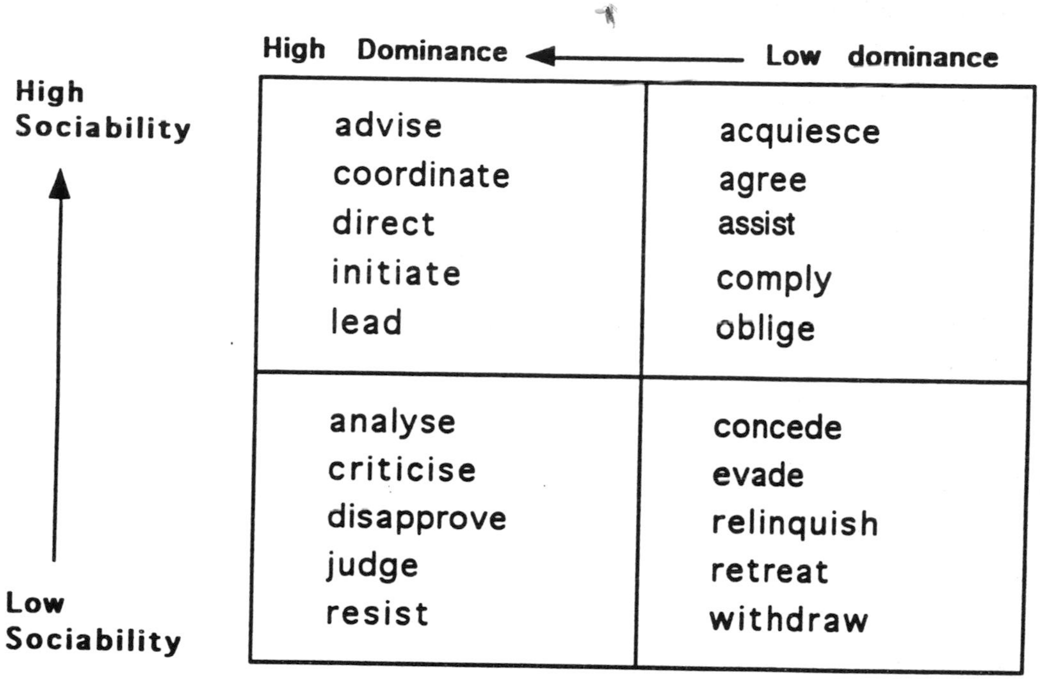

	High Dominance ←	Low dominance
High Sociability ↑	advise coordinate direct initiate lead	acquiesce agree assist comply oblige
Low Sociability	analyse criticise disapprove judge resist	concede evade relinquish retreat withdraw

Diagram: 5. Dominance / Sociability behavioural grid.

Most of us tend to rely for guidance on the teachings of our past experience in our dealings with others. Though useful, this particular kind of experience can be an imperfect information base at the best of times. Leaders wishing to improve their ability further in this field could consider studying some of the main elements of Transactional Analysis (T.A. for short). Despite its formidable title, T.A. provides a more understandable way for laymen to gain a better insight into human behaviour than an attempt to master psychology, which most of us have not the time to do. Regretfully, the nature of this essay can only extend to the inclusion of one or two sources about T.A. for further reading at the end of the book.

SECTION SIX

LEADER ATTITUDES AND APPROACHES

If the elements outlined in sections four and five are absorbed successfully into leading technique, an attitude and approach will develop over time that is rather different from that of the person who pursues an activity purely for personal satisfaction and pleasure. Keep in mind section one about aims and values.

clear or vague

Leaders need to have examined their own personal reasons and motives for wanting to take groups into the hills and to have clarified for themselves why they are wanting to do it at all, and to what ends. There needs to be a clear realisation that the responsibilities of leadership impose a discipline that allows very little room for personal wishes, ambitions or aspirations. Leadership in this context is a state of mind that is largely selfless.

Ego-trip

Leadership used for selfish ends is empty, non-creative and sterile. Leadership used to inflate the ego, such as needing to demonstrate personal expertise and "superior" powers to the group, is a destructive exercise without value to the group. The group should be approached with humility rather than arrogance. Leaders should not assume they always know what is best for the group or think they understand group needs so well that there is no need ever to consult them or ask for opinions. Leaders can not hope to pitch things at the group's level of expectation, motivation, interest and capability without some degree of consultation.

- A leader's interest in an activity should not over-shadow interest in the group. If getting into the hills or onto the water means more than leading a group, the leader should think twice before taking it on. If satisfactions are derived primarily from personal reasons such as so many miles covered, rivers descended or peaks ascended, a leader is going to be a disappointed, frustrated person who is unsympathetic to the group and a rotten leader. Very rarely will the motives, ambitions, interests and capabilities of the group coincide with that of the leader.

the technician

The leader's concept of the role should not consist solely of imparting as much technical know-how to the group as possible. There is more to the natural environment than teaching the skills and techniques of a particular sport. These technical crafts are essential aids and tools, but such a day so spent may be too clinical, too mechanical, and so without life. The essential nature of a mountain experience, for example, may be missed. Under the mass of time calculations, distances, bearings, conventional signs, contour lines, do's and don'ts, the mountains may be so obscured that they never have the chance to reveal their inherent attractions to the group. If the garnering of the leader's own experience was a chore, it may never be possible to generate an atmosphere in which a love and feeling for the outdoors can be transmitted to the group. Time should be given for the aesthetic and aye, maybe spiritual feelings, to impinge on the awareness of those in the group for whom such things will have meaning and great importance.

*" Time should be given for the aesthetic and, ...
......feelings to impinge on the awareness of the group."*

rigid or flexible

Some leaders find it necessary to impose a rigid structure on the group. Each person is given a place and number in a fixed order of march. This may be quite justifiable on a down-river canoe trip or a ski descent to discourage reckless competitive behaviour or overtaking in dangerous places. But where no deviation from the fixed order is permitted on a land based journey, the practice becomes questionable. Presumably such leaders either feel their responsibilities too acutely, or have an underlying anxious lack of self confidence in their ability to handle the fluidity of a group in the outdoors and feel a need to have a greater degree of containment about the situation. Hopefully this is an early stage that is passed through quickly. Such practice is sadly at variance with the freedom and informality of the outdoors. It is much more acceptable to see a group flowing freely and flexibly up a hillside path, interchanging according to the dictates of the social interaction going on within the group. The leader only needs to intervene when weather (mist) or difficult terrain require it. Often these factors will exert their own pressures on the group without the leader needing to say anything. There is no need to be rigid or precise about stops for 'breathers'. The group will not often permit it anyway, so why make things difficult?

Safe leadership will become what it ought to be, more a matter of good practice used discreetly so as to detract minimally from enjoyment.

•Another kind of rigidity is to be found in leaders who are unaware of the values which inform their attitudes and beliefs about approaches, leading styles, methods and what criteria constitute success. It is important for leaders to be able to distinguish between their personal values and the instrumental values which drive the aims of their courses or programmes. Instrumental values are of a different order or level and entail matters to do with:

- dependency
- independency (i.e. self-sufficient or not)

- interdependency (cooperation and collaboration),
- specialisation in depth (competence)
- width of experiences (tasting and group processes).

Unaware leaders tend to be single-minded and one- sided in their practice, for example, if a 'task' approach which values getting on with the activity as 'efficiently' as possible, is held dear, then an authoritarian, staff-centred style will be favoured. Such a style is characterised by directive, model-using methods because it is believed they are conducive to specialisation and thence lead to the high standards of skill and achievement so greatly to be desired. The leader who embraces these values unconsciously, registers a sharp antagonism when meeting the values implicit in the 'people' approach which is often perceived as being in opposition. This is largely because their own values, being unconscious, are felt to be the only ones in existence. Anything which appears to contradict those values is seen as an attack, not only on those values, but on the self which holds those values. It is felt that these are the only values that it is possible to hold and if these values were to be defeated or dismissed, nothing would be left. The resulting state of non-existence is not to be contemplated. Salvation lies in resistance.

It will be seen that unawareness tends to lead to a defensive rigidity and a correspondingly extremely polarised attitude which will be exclusive in the values it holds. An aware state assists a flexibility of outlook because it brings a realisation that such values need not be seen as mutually antagonistic elements, but as complementary assets to be used as matters of degree - each for their appropriate purpose.

Diagram: 6. illustrates the position.

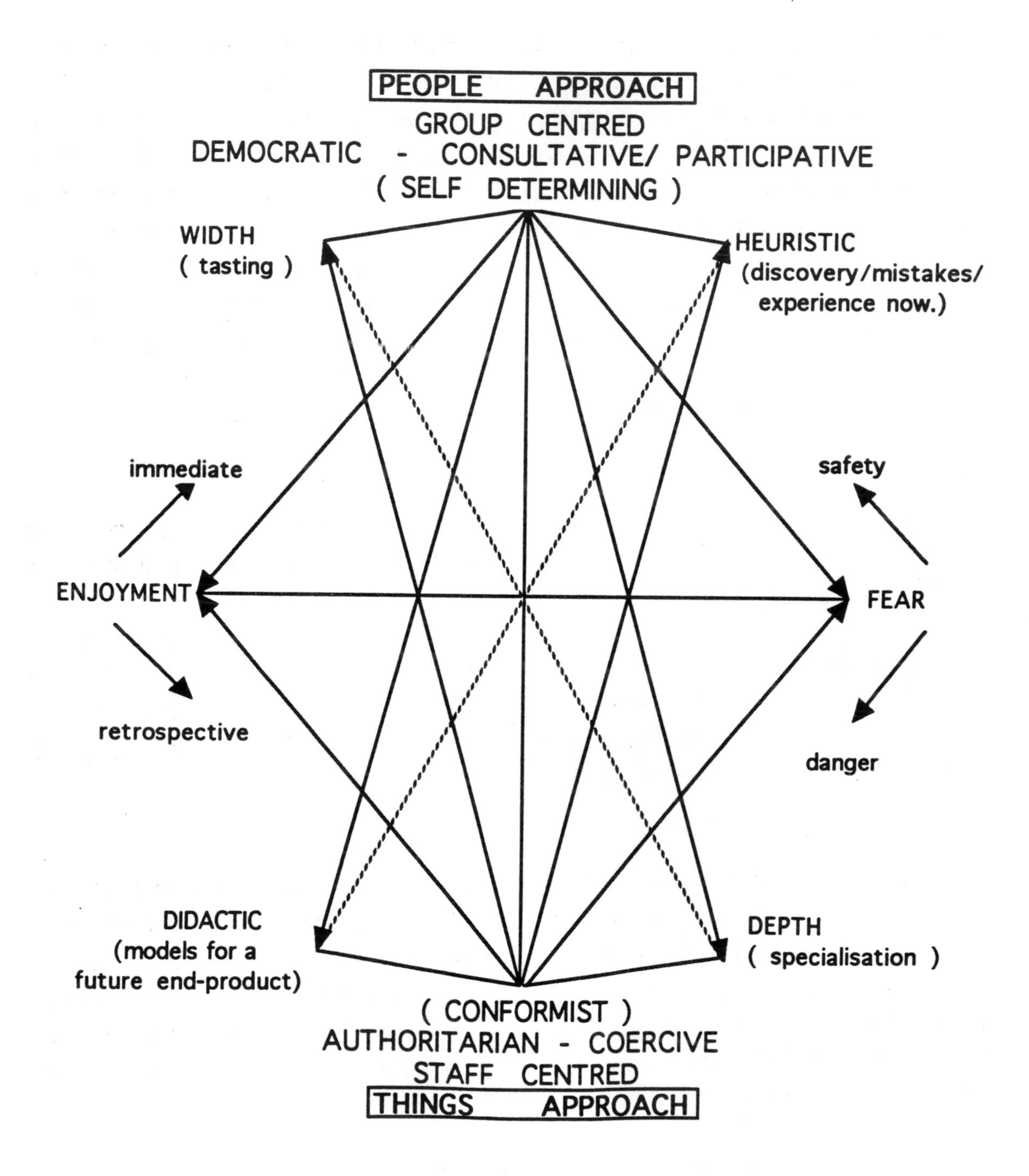

Diagram: 6. 'People' and 'Things' perspectives.

It is not necessary to think in terms of polarised opposites (as depicted by the dotted lines in the diagram).There are advantages to be gained by treating all these extremes as matters of degree. Embracing one of the approaches does not have to mean the outright rejection of the other. Thus in this diagram all the values most important to you are nearest to your chosen standpoint or orientation - towards either "people" or "things", i.e. task. Other less important values are not dismissed or ignored, but are placed further away and so are still valid and available to act as a complement as necessary. The fear-enjoyment axis is common to both orientations but may tend to acquire a particular value depending on which approach is acting upon it [15].

equipment talismen

Beware of the tendency of placing too much reliance and trust in equipment. However, carrying two of everything does not double the safety factor either.

Carrying equipment in duplicate results in a very heavy rucksack or canoe - a factor which in itself can affect safety margins. Part of the answer is to acquire the confidence that arises from good quality experience. One thing leaders can do in this respect is to carry a good repair kit as well as develop their improvisation skills.

outdoor magic

Colour, light and shade, shape and form, textures, sounds and scents are all part of the outdoor scene. Sometimes they will work their own magic unassisted and individuals will experience what has recently become known as "green adrenalin" - the exhilaration and excitement of experiencing high quality landscapes. Such feelings help create the reverential attitudes, referred to earlier, which are now needed to minimise environmental wear and tear.

At other times the leader may find it possible to heighten the group's awareness of them. The ability to interpret the natural landscape is of enormous value. Walking, for example, can be a monotonous business for many young people. They usually need to have been exposed to the hills a number of times before they come to appreciate that a good deal of the charm of mountains lies in their contrasts and infinite variety. Any snippet of information about flora, fauna, natural and man-made features, is grist to the leader's mill. Curiosity starved often dies quickly. Feed it and the results are often very surprising and fruitful. Beware of force feeding however.

environmental imperatives

The nature of the outdoor environment can sometimes be an over-dominating factor in the formation of a leader's attitude to group leading. The scenario goes like this: There are serious hazards in the mountains or on the water which imply harm will come to humans unless they modify the behaviour they normally adopt in man-made environments. Such modifications entail having the right equipment, skills and knowledge to cope, making sound preparations and taking proper precautions.

•These implications represent a set of imperatives which put serious responsibilities on leaders to ensure that all these requirements are met by their groups.
•So, the content of training programmes which leaders set up, will reflect these environmental imperatives.
•So also, the course of training, which is limited by a finite amount of time, will reflect these pressures on the leader to fulfil his/her responsibilities.
•Together, the environment, the training content and the course of training may constitute such a set of imperatives as are likely to be felt by a recipient group to be an authoritarian approach. The training tasks, the pace, the level, the pitch and the overall aims will have been set by externals that have no reference to, or origin in, the group's needs and capacities. Ironically, if a group should voice protest, the leader feels justified in ducking the 'flak' and responsibility by placing the blame for all the hassle on the environment.

expertise imperatives
Whereas in the illustration in the previous paragraph, the leader wished to distance him/herself from some of consequences of leadership by disclaiming responsibility for the less pleasant aspects, the opposite extreme is when leaders over mindful of their expertise, skills and status feel that they have a mandate to be authoritarian in all things. Because of all their expert training and extensive experience they think they know how to make the most of the possibilities of a situation and how best to use the time available. This conviction is even greater if they are faced with a group of volunteers, and even greater if the volunteers are unknowing novices. Such leaders may have made a number of erroneous assumptions about motives and expectations and may have neglected to take account of each individual's ability, fitness, needs, attitudes and background. In so doing, the ensuing low quality working relationships are likely to result in low achievement levels.

to impel or not to impel
There is one attitude common among leaders and outdoor practitioners in general, which needs a detailed examination. It is to do with aspects of the management of risk [16] and the belief expounded by Kurt Hahn that it is right to impel people into experiences. Whilst doubtless there are some occasions when this doctrine may be justifiable there are many, many more when it is not. In the wrong hands it can become a dangerous philosophy and all too easily be interpreted as a licence to dictate and to impose generally. It is needful to spend some time on the implications of this issue.
'Impelling' implies the use of compulsion and coercion by the impeller.

Between the extremes of silent apathy and open revolt, will be found all degrees of resentment, antagonism, hostility and resistance on the part of the impelled. The attitude receives some propping up from a school of ascetic thought which believes that "hair shirts and strength through pain" is a viable developmental approach. It is forgotten that the essence of this approach is that it should be voluntary. Whenever an element of unwillingness exists, positive consequences or outcomes are doubtful. Leaders are not sufficiently gifted with divine insight to enable them to predict whether they will be impelling their charges, both in the literal and metaphoric sense, in directions they do not want to go, at a speed they are unable to cope with, at a level they are not ready for, at an intensity that is too stressful to be beneficial. Just as importantly, leaders may run the risk of impelling people over their personal fear thresholds - which is the point beyond which fear ceases to have a useful survival function and becomes inhibitive, destructive, and even downright dangerous.

The business of pushing out personal limits and discovering them is an intensely personal and private matter. It is presumptuous and unethical for a leader even to contemplate doing it for someone else. It may happen incidentally and often does, especially during "epics" and emergencies; but to set out with the deliberate intention of doing so is a very questionable practice.

consequences-effects

A person who has an unpleasant experience, or who has failed in something into which s/he was impelled intentionally, can justifiably blame the 'impeller' for bad judgement and for the negative experience. Conversely, a person who has been allowed or encouraged to impel him/herself, and who fails or dislikes it, must undertake an internal evaluation to discover why. The responsibility for his/her own actions and development is still his/hers. It cannot be off loaded onto someone else. This self examination process in these circumstances leads to personal growth rather than diminishment.

• The success and enjoyment of a self impelled experience is of greater worth than that of the externally impelled. This is partly because of the need to go through the winding-up process required to generate the degree of motivation and commitment necessary to see the chosen task through. What you choose to do is a measure of what you think you can do. To do it and succeed confirms an estimate made of personal capacity - valuable self knowledge indeed. Success and achievement in self chosen activities imparts a greater degree of confidence and satisfaction than that derived from compulsory activities. Even if an impelled experience is enjoyed, it merely confirms the impeller's fortuitous estimation of the other person and does not really contribute much to gaining knowledge about the self.

When people are allowed a say or choice in decision making, their motivation and commitment tends to be higher and the nature of the activity is likely to be more closely related to their needs, abilities and capacities. Part of the leader's job is to help the group avoid the pitfalls of over or under-estimating their own abilities. Aspiration which exceeds capacity is doomed to disappointment and may be potentially dangerous. Under-achievement may be safer but sometimes can be worse than no achievement at all. Finding the right balance depends on the leader having sensitive communicating and negotiating skills so that challenges are pitched at the right level.

compromising ideals

An over zealous adherence to the ideals, principles and standards set by leader training courses can actually prevent youngsters from having any outdoor experiences at all. By 'following the book' and requiring their groups to come equipped with all that they are supposed to have, leaders automatically debar those who have not got it, cannot borrow or afford it. Leaders need to be prepared to compromise on these things but in such a way as not to compromise safety aspects. The nature of the day out needs to be adjusted in order that it is possible for the group to go on a trip that is not over-ambitious for the equipment they have. Take the old hoary problem of wearing tight fitting trousers on the mountain. Many youngsters may have nothing else. Possible solutions are to stay lower down or walk shorter distances. If a decent waterproof shell is available it is probably reasonable to go anyway, provided the forecast is not talking about strong winds and low or sub zero temperatures at three thousand feet.

The hazards of the natural environment do require one to take certain minimum precautions or be prepared to suffer the consequences of ignoring them. The threat of these consequences is always present to a greater or lesser degree. The insistent pressure of these environmental imperatives to conform to all the sound advice received in training make it difficult to go against it. Yet that is what the leader must do sometimes. The group will rarely ever be perfectly equipped, trained or fitted to cope with the objective perils. Leaders must know enough about their craft to be able to handle those situations where the reality of a situation requires the setting aside of the book of rules. This can be as much an ethical problem as it is a technical one. For example, " This scree filled gully that I have to descend with this group is of such a nature that all the usual recommended procedures are unsuitable. I think I can work out a safe way to do it but have I the right to commit this group to what is virtually an experiment?"

knots in relationships

Relationships in groups can sometimes assume a pattern best described as a circular 'knot' [17] akin to the 'chicken and the egg' idea. There seems to be no way out of an unbroken circular situation. Until it is broken, movement forward for the group is impossible. Here are some examples commonly found in groups:

- "I would like to have a say in what goes on. But I dare not speak out and say what I think. I might make mistakes and be laughed at or punished in some way. I do not want to be punished, so I will not try. So I do not get a say in what goes on."
- "I feel somebody always seems to be trying to pull me down. Others will take advantage and hurt or harm me in some way if I show I am weak (making mistakes) or vulnerable (at fault). I cannot trust anybody. So I must always try to protect myself against others by trying to keep on top, never admitting guilt or mistakes and never giving in. I would like it to be different but I cannot trust anybody because I'm always being got at."

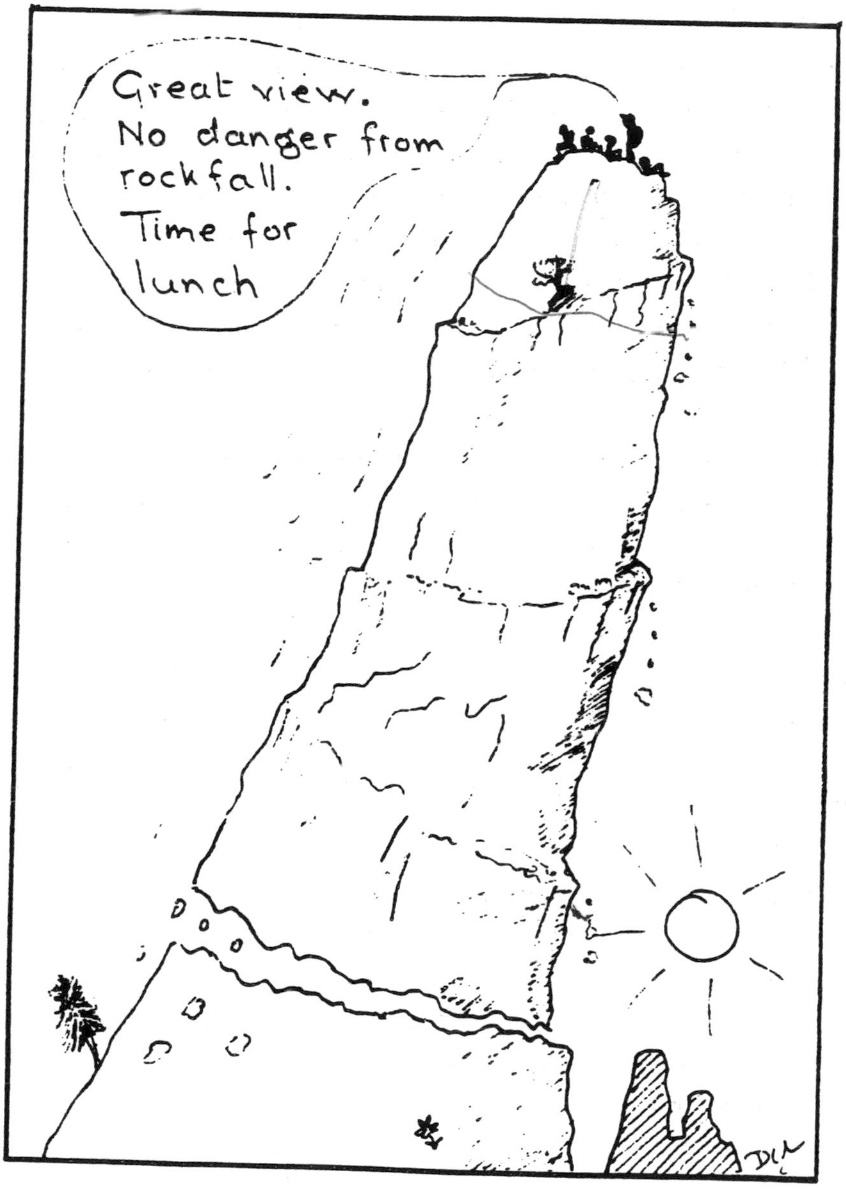

" The group will rarely ever be perfectly equipped, trained or fitted to cope with the objective perils."

• Another is when the group is looking to the leader for a lead or a decision even though there are no critical reasons for the pressure. Before responding to this pressure, it is worth trying to discern what these reasons are, especially if the leader wishes or needs to have a closer relationship with the group. There may be a genuine cause or it may be one of the classic games played by idle pupils on conscientious teachers. It is all too easy to succumb and 'do it all' for the group, especially if the leader is one of those who enjoy the dependence of others . In responding to this pressure the leader will most likely assume the conventional stereotype of what a leader is in the group's eyes. This may not be how the leader wants to be perceived by the group. But anxiety to produce answers the leader can feel the group expecting, will set her/him further apart. For in yielding to the pressure the leader will become directive. This knot is resolved by resisting the pressure and pushing responsibility for the problem back to the group where it can be shared with them. This tactic will help move them out of the habit of dependent mindedness and the abdication of responsibility towards a more resourceful and self sufficient attitude. Leaders can help people to want to be more responsible by helping them to feel they have a real say in what is going on, that their say is valued and by showing them that if they do not say their piece, resultant outcomes may not be to their liking.

need to be coherent, conscious, systematic

Because of the serious nature of the leader's responsibilities, the approach to the leadership situation must be systematic. The 'woolliness' of the "being with friends" situation referred to earlier, will no longer suffice. All the detailed factors relating to good practice, comfort and safety must be identified. In this context of safety, there must be a reason for everything done or said. The reason must be conscious. There will be many things learned in the early days by experience which are now done unconsciously without thought. For example, the way to walk and pick the way up or down a hill, or how to hold and use a paddle to keep a canoe in a straight line. All these things now have to be brought, as it were, from the back of the head to the front and consciously stored ready for use.

In those areas which relate to safety and comfort, leaders must be able to justify in minute detail everything they do or choose not to do.

This implies a very articulate grasp of the outdoor situation which only a process of reflective self-analysis and self-questioning about previous experience, outdoor and otherwise (both are relevant) will give. It is not enough to know the right thing to do. The leader must know why it is right and what the consequences will be if it is done incorrectly or differently.

SECTION SEVEN

LEADERSHIP SKILLS

Implicit in all that has been said so far about leadership, are a number of general functions specifically pertinent to the exercise of leadership. These are some of the more important ones:

functions of the leader [3]

1. To take responsibility.
2. To control.
3. To care for.
4. To support.
5. To set and maintain standards and limits.
6. To make decisions.
7. To make decisions about how decisions are made.
8. To sustain the group's energy.
9. To engage and commit personal energy to the group's achievement of its task.
10. To be aware of and be able to respond appropriately to the reality of:
    - the task.
    - the group in your charge.
    - the individual differences in the group.
11. To be aware of and responsive to:
    - your own feelings, wants and needs.

- the feelings, wants and needs of the group as a whole and its individual members.

To carry out these functions effectively, a leader needs to be able to call on a range of both technical (task orientated) skills and relationship (people orientated) skills. The technical skills are to be found elsewhere in other books or manuals. Section seven focuses on some of the more important "people" skills which are trainable skills and which can be acquired to assist the leader in the function of leading. Indeed, the attempt should be made so to develop these skills that they become ingrained habits rather than skills.

attitudes/prejudices causing learning difficulties

Much of the information that follows throughout this section is abstract in nature and is of the kind that is intangible and therefore difficult to pin down. But it is so much a part of everyday life that it is taken-for-granted. The obvious often goes unseen. If before reading about them, you were asked to make a list of these leader skills, describe them or the processes of which they are a part, say how they are used and what their significance is, you might find it quite difficult to do. But as you read about them they will seem to be so familiar that you will think you already know them. In a way you do. You use them every day. But your use of them may have been largely reactive or subconscious. As a leader your use of them will need to be more proactive and consciously deliberate. An effort of memorisation and practice is required before some of them will be effectively absorbed into your usual way of doing things.

In the U.K., especially in sport or adventure type activities, because the accent tends to be on "doers" and achievers, there has built up some prejudice about getting involved in the intricacies of leadership skills (see remarks in the introductory section). There is a fairly widespread deficit in the possession of, or belief in the value of, inter-personal skills. "Psychology and all that " is one way, and a mistaken one, of

how the field of inter-personal skills tends to be perceived and is thus seen as rather intellectual or esoteric and remote from the job of leading. It is argued here that leadership should be informed by a good knowledge and understanding of people. When a leader is not so informed, an unaware state will tend to render leadership formless or rudimentary, insensitive or unskilled, and prone to ill considered acts likely to arouse conflict.
There are perhaps, lessons to be learned from this country's long history of discord and strikes in the relationships between the labour force and management which has too frequently accentuated getting on with the task and neglected the good relationships required to get the job done.
Interestingly, management training and development is a growth industry these days.

Another source of resistance possibly arises from the image of thinking, sensitive leadership being perceived as not quite 'masculine' enough or 'practical' enough for the majority of British leaders who are male. For reasons to do with the cultural mores of our society which imposes assumptions on, and prescribes behaviour for women and girls, female participation in outdoor activities generally and in mountain activities in particular, has been much less in extent and not as varied as that of male involvement. The majority of participants being male in this field means a preponderance of male values with the accent on technical excellence (i.e. competence) and achievement (i.e. task).
Probably, because it too is imposed by society, women tend to be better at the 'people' skills and men better at the 'technical' skills. Is it possible that men subconsciously deduce from this that the relationship skills are feminine and therefore to be kept at a distance in order to avoid being branded by their peers as womanish? The terminology currently in use to describe technical skills as 'hard' and the inter-personal, relationship skills as 'soft' is misleading, crude and idiomatic. It does not seem to help a proper discernment, recognition and acceptance by the male community.

A more productive line of approach would be to use the term "technical skills" for so-called 'hard skills' and apply as appropriate, the terms "inter-personal skills" or "leadership skills" for so-called 'soft skills'.

gender issues: male:female differences

Discussion about 'gender images' above, leads to a consideration of the part played by gender differences in outdoor activities. What do leaders need to know about gender to do their job more effectively? The next few sub-sections on this topic can only lightly touch a large subject and essay to highlight a few of the more important issues. I am also conscious that anyone attempting to write on this topic enters a minefield. But the subject has to be addressed in an attempt to establish some guidelines for dealing satisfactorily with mixed groups. Difficulty is no excuse for avoidance.

Whether with a mixed group, or an all female or all male group, it is essential for a leader to take into account certain fundamental differences between the sexes. To ignore them, will be to allow all manner of injustice, resentment, alienation and opting out to take place.

The biological differences are obvious, but until the onset of puberty, the other physiological differences are less marked and the sexes are almost equal in physical ability. Thereafter, boys in the main are heavier built and stronger than girls. Beyond this point the way in which these differences are overlain with other mis-applied meanings, creates a whole mish-mash of misinterpretations and misconceptions. 'Stronger' suddenly becomes 'better' or 'superior'. 'More powerful' becomes 'domineering' and 'over-powering'. Power values for weight-strength ratios are discounted as are the benefits of being "light" or having a low centre of gravity. There are curious contradictions too! The 'weaker' sex is expected to be able to lift a three year old and a full shopping bag or a bedridden parent. Such feats or tasks are conveniently dismissed by male outlooks as "women's work".

<u>boys</u>

From birth, boys are bombarded by a set of attitudes which anachronistically hark back to the values of those times when food had to be hunted and territory or possessions defended. There was a need to be hard, aggressive and brave in order to succeed. Rearing methods still teach boys to strive to be strong mentally as well as physically. "Be a man!" "Don't cry". "If he hits you, hit him back". "Do not show weakness". If he cannot do these things, adult disdain reveals to him that he is not a real boy. So to prove he is a boy he has to try to do these things. In all boys' groups, in times of stress, disagreement or conflict, these pressures are at work, elevating or degrading (depending on your point of view) their collective behaviour into one resembling the law of the jungle. To survive you have to prove yourself by showing that you cannot be taken advantage of. It is important not to appear vulnerable, so mistakes, or feelings of being incompetent or inadequate, cannot be voiced or admitted. To be put down or discounted is not to be countenanced. To "get somewhere" in such a climate, you have to prove yourself worthy of a place in the pecking order. To do that you have to enter a competition, either at least to stay off the bottom, or at most to reach the top of the pile. Desire to belong in the peer group creates a strong compulsion to conform to this way of behaving. It is an unusual or strong personality that can resist the pressure of this ethos and go his own way. Needless to say, ways of operating in this maelstrom, vary from the raw, naive, blatant use of crude physical aggression to subtle, obscure, cunning, psychological manipulation.

A subsidiary, but no less important, theme of this essay is the need for male leaders to devote more time to getting across to boys that "being a man" does not mean acting out all those behaviours that our culture has indoctrinated males into believing are the socially approved ways to behave.

"Maleness" is too often perceived to be all about proving oneself by being competent, doing things and showing off to females, coming out on top by being aggressive and competitive, never admitting to vulnerability (being perfect,. never making mistakes) nor admitting to being or feeling inadequate or incompetent in case it is taken advantage of and exploited to the detriment of oneself.

"Manliness" on the other hand is all about leaving most of this immature, adversarial stuff behind and growing out of it. It is to do with helping rather than fighting; cooperating with others; taking more account of the less strong, or those in a minority; coming down off the power driven pedestal of fear and refraining from indulging in all those non-productive behaviours such as the down-putting, point-scoring antics and the combative wasteful tactics that males of all ages engage in too frequently.

To convert boys' groups from these culturally determined inclinations is no easy matter. They live in a competitive world and it would be a mistake to try to eliminate competitiveness completely from their personalities. What has to be attempted is their acceptance of the idea that a total dependence on this adversarial style of strategy as a way of life is undesirable. In the long run it is inefficient and wasteful - witness the combative exhibition we see daily in Parliament! They have to be convinced that it is unworthy and immature. They need to be shown that there are alternative viable ways of behaving and relating to others that can be equally effective in achieving aims.
A simple exercise can give an invaluable insight into the thoughtless way males tend to operate. Place a group of boys in a circle facing inward with their arms linked tightly together. Then ask the one boy you have kept out of it to try to get into the circle by any means he can devise. The resulting spectacle is illuminating. It usually becomes a violent attack/defend test of brute force. Rarely does the outsider resort to subtler methods. Positive, straight tactics such as a civil request or an appeal to friends are never given a thought.
Whilst not all male leaders exhibit the macho characteristics of

maleness as it has been culturally determined in Western societies, a sufficiently high proportion of them, and the boys in their groups, do. Age-old attitudes which support this male stance, may hinder the acceptance of ideas which challenge the customs and practice characterised by male behaviour.

Leaders' resistance, for example, to the acquisition of relationships skills can be overcome. They may have the belief that being outdoors is 'good' for young people but may not have thought through how that 'goodness' comes about. Such leaders can be compared to the vague mystic who relies on faith or random chance to produce desired results. This is not very professional. Most of the 'good' outcomes that are looked for in young people, arise out of the inter-active, inter-personal processes that go on in groups. These need time and space to emerge, develop and flourish. The only way to make this potential 'good' more probable is to avoid using leadership styles that inhibit group interaction and to use styles that actively promote it. The traditional directive style of leadership at best damps down, at worst paralyses, such interaction because it is over concerned with the activity and the skills needed to do it. Certain styles which can guarantee that issues will arise, are those which rely on interaction between people for success, i.e. the democratic, participatory, delegatory styles of leadership. They do not attempt to predict specific outcomes but they do ensure that there will be the supportive contexts or favourable climates necessary for their existence. This is what will ensure that desired outcomes receive their due in time and attention.

By using these styles, the opportunity for personal development and effectiveness is structured into a programme - it is no longer a matter of optimism or chance.

girls

Girls have developed alternative strategies for achieving their objectives. I enter this arena with some trepidation and a wish not to be seen as patronising. I hope I succeed. As a male I cannot really speak about an all girls' group when no males are present, but since their physical abilities would be equal, relatively speaking, I could imagine that sometimes conflicts might not be too dissimilar to an all boys' group. The struggle for a place in the pecking order may, or may not be, as physical and though the quality of the psychological warfare may be quite refined it could be just as vicious!
In general girls could quite probably be a lot stronger physically than they actually are . But they are like boys, in that the manner of their upbringing is culturally determined too, but along different lines. Girls are exhorted to take care of themselves in case "they hurt themselves", the underlying (never mentioned but implied) concern being to ensure that the reproductive capacity is unimpaired. So girls learn early not to get wet or muddy or do dangerous things. One noticeable offshoot of this is an observed unwillingness for girls to make big, massive movements, as for example when scrambling over rock. It seems to stem not so much from a sense of physical inadequacy as from a wariness not to be over exposed to a commitment to danger. It may also be the early consequence of wearing a dress which tends to inhibit big movements.

From an early age, girls observe and experience what it is like to lack either power or physical strength. Later in life as mothers, the job of looking after children places them in a vulnerable position. Without the benefits of power, alternative ways need to be found to achieve what they want and these strategies are passed on to the next generation. So negotiation and cooperation, the only method available to them when you think about it, has developed as the favoured method. Along with cooperative negotiation come all the other skills and qualities concerned with persuasion, tolerance, consideration, sympathy and compassion. Is it little wonder that women appear to outshine men in the sphere of interpersonal skills? For this reason it is quite common for many male leaders to prefer to have all female groups. Not because they may be more biddable, indeed often they may not be, but because there is less hassle in the group amongst its members which makes it pleasanter to be with and easier to relate to.

<u>mixed groups</u>

Problems of a particular kind tend to arise in mixed groups when the time is spent battling on unequal terms. If the brash, aggressive, adversarial behaviour of insecure boys is allowed to obtain, if their compulsion to prove themselves is allowed to prevail, choices about activities will tend to reflect their male preoccupations with physical strength, stamina, and courage. Competitiveness about skill competence is also likely to be present and it may even be compounded by the presence of girls in one or two ways. The boys may perceive it as an opportunity to show off their paces to the opposite sex in an attempt to impress them and appear more attractive. If these influences are allowed to run unchecked, most girls will find themselves constrained to operate at a disadvantage. Naturally they will not like it and will lose interest, or as a response to this enforced powerlessness, 'egg' the boys on in order to gain some sense of effectiveness from the situation. Girls tend to have a different approach to life. Taught by nurture and experience to be less assertive or aggressive, they are just as likely to decide not to join the dismal fray and stand back to remain uninvolved, letting the boys get on with it, possibly resentful but certainly not impressed. In such circumstances they are likely to feel let down, cheated of justice, even betrayed by the authority figure in which they have had to place their trust. Their seeming passivity (I nearly wrote 'seething passivity', which I have no doubt it often is) may go unnoticed by a leader, who may be either insensitive to their reactions, or too personally involved himself in the power struggles to rise above them. Attention regretfully, often stays focussed on the disrupters, the noisy ones with a lot to say, the extroverts and those who seem to know what they want.

<u>gender implications and consequences</u>

The style of debate adopted by males, is usually characterised by posturing, boasting and position-taking. Because it closes off the possibility of flexibility, open-mindedness, the ability to change your mind, express doubt, or admit you were wrong, it is unsuited to the female disposition. It often deliberately creates an intimidating environment that discourages dialogue of the kind with which girls feel most comfortable. Girls are good at listening because they tend to be interested in what is happening, and boys are good at interrupting because they see it as a battle for "air time". Whoever gets to talk longest, wins.

Female silence is greatly misinterpreted by males. If it is taken to mean ignorance, intelligent girls are likely to find themselves being told what to think by boys whom they may perceive as their intellectual inferiors. If it is construed to mean uncertainty or indecision, things will be decided for them. More silence will be conveniently seen as consent.[18] Should the silence be broken by protesting or accusatory girls, the boys will be unable to treat it seriously because they cannot handle it and will take cover behind appeals to logic and attempts to deride emotional outbursts. "You are being childish." "You are too emotional- you must try to be more rational." "You are not being at all reasonable." This sort of denial of feelings can be very corrosive in its effect on relationships in a mixed group.

Perhaps because they feel they do not have as much face to lose as do the boys and because they operate mostly in the cooperative mode, it is easier for girls to confess when they feel unable to do something or express doubts about their ability or competence. Sometimes girls, who are only too aware that this kind of behaviour is perceived by boys as "being feminine", make use of it as a tactic. This seeming lack of confidence is often construed by males as inadequacy or incompetence when in fact girls are just as capable as the boys. The difference is that boys, who are likely to be just as uncertain about themselves, will rarely if ever admit to feelings of inadequacy for fear of a loss of status in the group. There are rare times when leader intervention enables a mixed group to see beyond the customary masks. When each sex sees in the other a mirror image of its own fears and anxieties, meaningful dialogue ensues.

It will be apparent that in the context of teamwork and groups, boys and girls labour under a plethora of disabilities in the realm of personal skills. It is a wonder anything ever gets done. Achievements are likely to be at no little cost to some in the group in terms of self respect and a sense of personal identity. Girls are more likely to be used to and skilled at compromise and negotiation. Cooperation depends upon it. [19]

" Female silence is too often misinterpreted by males"

need for leader intervention

Parity of opportunity, either in discussion time, or in choosing activities, or in decision-making will not occur unless the leader takes positive action to ensure that conditions are conducive for parity to take place.

It is worth emphasising this truth for the simple reason that it lies at the heart of the issues surrounding the futures of young people themselves and the nature of their development. It is as much about whether they themselves will derive maximum benefit, as whether the potential of the outdoor experience itself will be fully utilised, which is at stake.

• Leaders, male and female, can do much in providing, by their own example, good positive role-models from which both sexes can learn.

women leading all-male groups

A note about women who have to lead all-male groups might be useful at this point. The remarks that follow are probably more observable with, and applicable to, all-male groups coming from inner city contexts. As with all generalisations, not every all-male group will exhibit this type of reaction.

The normal expectation of boys involved in some kind of outdoor activity is that a male will lead them in their sessions. When this does not happen and a woman appears before them, their ideas about leader role-models in the outdoors receives a jolt. The severity of reaction may range from mild surprise to outrage. Some may feel that they are being sold short; some will feel that they are doomed to soft options - there is a sense of some kind of betrayal at work. At bottom is the feeling that "women don't do these things as well as men so we won't have as good a time as we should." These feelings of disappointment and/or resentment will show themselves in a variety of ways all designed to test out and discover the mettle of the leader, whether this woman leader is worthy of respect and of course, who will be the boss. Leaders of such groups can expect, cheek, overt disobedience, attempts to knock the leader off-track by hustling her through induction processes at a hurried pace, arguing with the leader's proposals or decisions, brisk questioning of her actions. The strategies required to cope with or counter this sort of situation will be as varied as the leaders themselves. The reaction of an all-male group to a woman leader will be dependent partly on how the group perceives that individual. The first impressions and initial conclusions they draw about her will determine what form their action takes. Is she attractive or not, young or not, athletic or academic looking, and so on? So it cannot be the purpose of this essay to give answers on this one but simply to flag its existence and the need to have thought out ways of dealing with it. A leader faced with this situation in an unprepared condition would be in for a bad time, not to mention the possible dangerous spin-offs that could accrue whilst pursuing potentially dangerous activities. Suffice it to say that the leader has to find means to impose her personality on the group to the point that gains their respect without antagonism - not easy to do and sometimes unavoidable. It is likely that a stand will have to be taken sooner or later about something. Very few women leaders win through on charm alone. So if a stand has to be taken, it would seem prudent for the leader to be aware what sort of ground she is strong on and herself choose the terms of any confrontation.

categorising skills

The need to categorise skills and the skill to be able to categorise, should not be regarded merely as an academic luxury but as a crucial aid to assist leaders in the task of internalising a mass of information so that it can be more easily handled, managed and used.
Various ways of categorising and classifying the 'relationship' skills are possible [3]. In time leaders should find their own and better ways to do this.

The relationship skills required by a leader for operating effectively could be listed under three general headings:

Communication Skills	Group management Skills	Assertion Skills
Listening	Planning	Influencing
Expressing	Organising	Controlling
Informing	Decision making	Positive assertion
Questioning	Supervising	Confronting
Clarifying	Monitoring	Responding to criticism
Facilitating	Mediating	Directing

Skills could also be classified according to the object on which they are used:

- the self: which is personal.
  e.g. self analysis or self awareness.

- others: which is interpersonal as in one to one relationships.
  e.g. feeding back.

- others as a whole: which is the group and one relating to many.
  e.g. briefing, summarising, managing.

Skills could be categorised by their type or nature:

- awareness skills: such as looking, listening, sensing and intuiting which is:
  -to do with knowing what is going on .

- understanding skills: such as analysing, diagnosing, inducting, deducing and prognosticating which implies having the necessary models, pertinent concepts and sensitive perception which is:
  -to do with understanding what is going on - in order to know what to do next.

- adaptive skills: such as having a range of real behavioural choices. Being aware of and able to control personal feelings will help to avoid being locked into one style of leading for example.

Simon Priest's 'PEOPL' model [20] looks at the whole picture and classifies skills in another way under eight separate headings. These are :

-Safety skills:
-Technical Activity skills:
-Organisational skills:
-Environmental skills:
-Instructional skills:
-Group Management skills:
-Problem Solving skills:
-Flexible leadership skills: i.e. the ability to use all styles appropriately.

All these classification devices are but tools to assist leaders with the identification and integration of them into personal practice. Only when they are known about, can they be built up into a usable framework, to be then fleshed out, improved and amended by experience. There is not space fully to do that here. In any case it is preferable that leaders evolve their own ways of meshing them into an interrelated, integrated structure. It will be the one that is understood best. Filling out of some of the more significant skills follows below, but for the most part the intention is mainly to raise levels of awareness about them and give some indication of their range, scope, depth and importance.

planning and forethought - anticipation

Accidents are often the result of simple omissions arising out of poor planning and weak preparation. Prevention is better than having to find a cure. Good planning eradicates at a stroke, many potential causes of trouble. Perusal of the annual reports of rescue units quickly provides affirmation of this point. Many incidents occur through the neglect of some very basic precaution such as ensuring that suitable footwear is worn or equipment checked before use.

Planning is a skill which will enable leaders to meet difficulties in a greater state of preparedness. It will often provide them with a ready made course of action when emergencies arise and will mean that the necessary resources to meet them are to hand too. It is of course, undesirable to go about continually expecting crisis after crisis. But it is wise to be ready for them when they happen and have a rough plan of action already prepared to meet them.

Typical examples would be, "What equipment am I likely to need on this expedition I am planning", or, " If someone had an accident here, what would I do?" And, "If something happened to me could the group cope?" Alternatively, " If I had to take this group down there, how long would it take and who would be the ones to watch?" Or, "Where is the point of no return on this trip?"

• But beware of over-planning and over-preparation. There is a point beyond which it chokes spontaneity both in the leader and the quality of the experience for the group. Be willing and able to flex and change when it is advantageous to do so.

• One easily overlooked piece of forethought is keeping a group informed about where it is, where it is headed and what are some of the names of the places, peaks and passes. Groups are very soon disorientated if they have not been very involved in the planning of a journey. Not really knowing where you are can be very disturbing. Knowing a few names gives the comforting illusion of making strange ground seem familiar. If one of the group should become detached or lost, both leader and the lost will lose face when it becomes apparent that the strayer did not know whether s/he was in Langdale or Llanberis.

It can be as basic as that.

" Where is the point of no return on this trip ?"

planning in highlights

All leaders want their groups to have enjoyable experiences. This causes some leaders to try to plan into the programme what they call "positive" experiences. They also plan to avoid negative ones. It should be noted that though this is laudable and understandable, it is impracticable. The old dictum that "One man's meat is another man's poison" has an application in the outdoors. An individual's perception about what constitutes adventure or enjoyment is quite subjective and personal to the extent that "one person's challenge may be another

person's despair." Some will revel in the challenge and exhilaration of wild, wet days, rocky scrambles or long treks into remote places. Others will be turned off or frightened by dark, wet, cold caves or the look of very turbulent waters when afloat.
A look at some of the types of risk found in adventure experiences will be useful since assumptions about what constitutes risk/adventure are often narrow [16].

types of risk

Many practitioners in the outdoors tend to see the risk purely in terms of physical risk. But a list of most of the 'bad consequences' of risk shows that risk may entail danger to the 'thinking' self and the 'feeling' self as well as the 'physical' self.
All risks represent a threat to basic human needs as listed by A.H.Maslow [5] (see section four). Knowledge of these needs is a useful tool in helping to identify just what kind of risks are being run in a particular course of action. With reference to those needs, here are a few of the sort of risks that may be involved at any time.

1. On a *physical survival* level, loss of health, injury or death, could be caused by risk to food supply, shelter, rest and medicine - as well as accidents or mishaps.

2. At the level of *physical security needs* , loss of property, money, valuables or equipment represent " material" kinds of risks.

3. On a higher level, the *need for self esteem* could be threatened by running the risk of being exposed to mockery, ridicule, disapproval and worst of all, loss of credibility. The possibility of being 'put down', 'discounted' or ignored is a fierce inhibitor/motivator. In asserting oneself to register or maintain one's position, or to avoid being left defenceless or vulnerable, one may run the risk of being given responsibility, of being held responsible and accountable, of being in the wrong, of being betrayed even.

It is a fine point whether it is worse to lose face in one's own eyes or to lose it in the eyes of others - one's peers in particular for example, which brings in the next set of needs.

4. There are *needs of a social security kind* such as a sense of belonging, of being valued by others (prestige), of being part of a community without losing one's sense of being different. These could be threatened by the risk of rejection and possible eviction from the group, resulting in loss of status and companionship. Staying in the group might mean a risk of losing a sense of independence. On the other hand, standing up for what one believes in could attract the hostility that loses friends; could attract the attention or the responsibilities a present level of self confidence could not cope with; could attract the scorn or ridicule one's self esteem could not tolerate. The need to be understood and the risk of being misunderstood are uncomfortable bedfellows.

5. It would appear that all risk is ultimately related to whatever supports or constitutes a person's *sense of identity* and need for it. This includes the highest set of needs to do with a *sense of purpose* and the *values* associated with it.

It should be apparent that the perception of emotional risk in a situation can be just as powerful, or more, in its effect on individuals in a group, as is the possibility of physical hurt.

Experiences can usually only be classed as positive or negative *after* the event, not before it. It cannot therefore be predicted or planned. The devices and tactics planned by leaders to increase enjoyment, excitement or interest and to decrease stress, discomfort and anxiety, may not always have their planned effect. Leaders have to try to do these things sometimes, succeeding more often than not, but they also need to monitor and test on-going group responses in case unintended effects indicate a need for a change of approach.

The most obvious change to be made is to reduce the assuming and presuming done by the leader in favour of more testing and consulting.

managing risk

In addition it is as well to be aware that the risk-taking capacity of the person managing the risk elements of a situation is an important consideration in the management of risk. It is sometimes the over-riding determinant in a situation. In this sense, the management of risk is all about the leader's character and not at all about the leader's technical ability to weigh numbers in the group against difficulties of terrain or to manipulate equipment carried, skill and experience against some natural hazard or obstacle . Risk-taking that is the result of too much courage, pride or rash bravado and too little judgement is reckless, foolhardy and probably accident prone. Too little courage and too much humility, thinking and consideration can result in over caution and not a lot of learning. Finding the right balance is all-important.
In the dictionary definition, all the consequences of risk are negative and bad. It is interesting that educational practice in the outdoors contradicts this dictionary view and regards the outdoors as a risk medium which may lead to positive outcomes such as increased confidence, self knowledge and social awareness.
When thinking about example situations in an attempt to become clear in one's mind about this, one can get in quite a confused state trying to decide which is the risk, which is the challenge, and which is the fear.

A few definitions may help to sort things out here.

- Challenge is something that confronts you which you choose to do.
  You may or may not be sure you can do it.

- Risk is the consequence if you can not do it.

- Fear may be about either or both of these.

• Pay-off is the dividend or benefit expected if the challenge is met successfully.

Motivation is generated by the self internally when measuring the balance between risk and the inducements of the pay off. Pay-off is thus allied closely to motivation. But motivation can also be provided by external events outside one's control, e.g. a prize or some other thing that may be attractive or even vital, like a train to be caught or a pursuing avalanche. It can be stimulated by some one else, but thereafter the motivation has to become yours or one enters the realm of compulsion.

<u>checking</u>

Cultivate this skill until it becomes a habit.

• Check that both the leader and the group have the necessary food, clothing and equipment before setting off. In a concern for others, leaders should beware of forgetting to check that their own gear is complete. It happens sometimes.

• Check that any instructions given, are heard, understood and obeyed. This is obvious and should be basic, but it is often neglected, particularly in the informal, fluid circumstances that are characteristic of parties outdoors. Noise from strong winds, rain on anorak hoods, rushing rivers or streams, inattention simply caused by the distraction of people moving about are features common to many types of outdoor situation; they all affect the hearing quite considerably.

• Check how things are going with the party. With practice this becomes a 'sense' that is always 'switched on'. If the leader is at the front, there should be frequent looking back. It is so easy to forge on unaware of the mounting chaos behind.

observation, perception and interpretation

These skills are supplementary to the habit of checking. Together they constitute the foundation of the leader's system of control. The leader needs to know what is going on around - in the environment and in the group. Seeing and checking what is going on gives that knowledge. The ability to perceive things varies greatly in people. Work to improve it. This is one of those skills where, if it is desired hard enough, it will happen.

• But be aware that observation and its co-partner, perception, is often selective too. Like a self-fulfilling prophesy, one often only sees what one expects, or wants to see. Try to avoid tuning to particular wave-lengths, as it were, and keep the 'receiver' wide open. In practice this means not jumping too quickly to conclusions about what you see or what will happen. This is not as easy as it sounds. Being 'tuned' to everything is rather like being tuned to nothing and akin to the feeling of being switched off. Learn to distinguish between the two states. Listen for the 'static'!

• Perception is followed by an almost compulsive process of interpretation, a desire to assign meaning to what is observed. It is too easy to make a prediction and jump to conclusions. This is an area of moral ground where it is difficult to know whether to judge an action by the intention that caused it or by the effect it produced. When observing behaviour, people tend to interpret and judge it on the grounds of what they see or feel - the effect it has on them or the consequences it has for other people. What they do not see often are the causes of that behaviour or the motives that drove it. These can often put things in a very different light. Sometimes hostility between people in a group bursts out in violence. The leader sees furniture broken, tents torn, or others kept awake by the din. In the heat of the moment, incorrect motives may be read in to the events observed. It may seem on the face of it to be one of many varieties of delinquent behaviour - wanton damage, mindless violence, vandalism, bullying, inconsiderate anti-social behaviour.

" It may seem..........to be one of the many varieties of delinquent behaviour "

It is important to find out the real reason. It may not have been aggression on the offensive, but prove to have been a defensive, inner act of survival, or a reaction to severe provocation. The link between cause and effect is often quite different from what one imagines it to be. The trick is to avoid being too judgmental too early and, providing circumstances permit, allow more time for things to reveal their true nature.

The practical point for leaders here is that just as their judgement skills in more concrete, physical situations in the outdoors can be improved, so can their skills in relationships situations be honed by keeping simple records for a time about their impressions and expectations of events occurring in their groups and the decisions and actions to which those events gave rise.

• It is mainly by observation that a leader will get to know the characteristics, strengths and weaknesses of each member of the party. Although a lot of chat may be exchanged with the group, it is the non-verbal sounds, facial expressions and body signals that will provide the needed knowledge about conditions in the group. Mainly by observation will the leader become aware of signs of tiredness, boredom, low morale, tension, anxiety stresses, personality conflicts, acute discomforts, feelings of insecurity, lack of a sense of balance, lack of powers of coordination, sloppy, energy- consuming footwork and so on. All these signs and many others leaders will usually have to discern for themselves, for the members of the group will tend not to want to say anything about them. The pressure of a group on the move for example, is a palpable thing and may cause people within the group to feel reluctant to slow it down, or stop it. The leader may have to find out by asking direct questions. It is a simple matter to give them an opening by making it clear that their comfort or enjoyment is as equally important as pushing on.

• The need to keep observing the environment is basic and should be obvious. Continuously assess its implications for the party in terms of enjoyment and pleasure, danger and effort. On land, assess the terrain and which routes offer most interest, protection from head winds, reasonable footing - not always footpaths which may be badly eroded, or dotted with greasy rocks or interrupted by unbridged streams requiring to be crossed. Watch out for changes in the weather such as mist on land or fog at sea; and particularly for water borne activities, be aware of changes in the strength or direction of the wind, rising water levels and accelerating currents, tidal or otherwise.

coaching and supporting

Unless you come from a P.E. background, leaders tend to be conditioned by the way training schemes in their chosen activity treat the skill of coaching and how a person acquires a skill. You tend to teach in the way you were taught.

Historically, the received body of wisdom regarding the theory and practice of the acquisition of skill exists within the public sector of education, in Physical Education. But amateur governing bodies of outdoor sports were not a part of this. Without access to, or disregarding developments in currently accepted theory, these bodies tended to become outdated and insular in their approach to skill coaching. Operating from the naive belief that the quickest way to achieve proficiency and competence in a skill is the method that appears to be the most direct and straightforward way, they put their belief in traditional, didactic, directive methods. Most coaching methods geared to improving physical performance conformed to this model. I remember BCU coaches horrified at the sight of 'play' approaches to skill sessions and failing instructors under test for an award for using them. The ski school is the classic stereotype of the approach with its stylised regimentation and pursuit of the perfect "end form" movement. The RYA has its official 'method' for teaching sailing.

Things are changing however, and there is for example, a book of games designed specifically to improve canoeing skills. But the residual net effect of the past on many leaders is that the process of coaching a skill is assumed to be purely physical in nature. Sometimes it is, but sometimes it is not. Olympic Coaches for example, now place considerable emphasis on their athletes developing powers of concentration.

In situations where people are experiencing difficulty or distress, the reason or cause of that is often not obvious. It is therefore hard for a leader to decide what the right kind of assistance should be. Because of this, the skills of coaching and supporting are often poorly executed. Analytical observation or remembering past experience and feelings can often help a decision about what kind of help to give. How often is advice given about walking skills when ascending and especially descending? If it is given, is it given to everybody or only to those in need who are making heavy weather of it? How much use is the advice to "try and keep a rhythm", or "try to conserve energy"? In these cases the need is to give the person a tip about *"how to do it"*. Advice must mean something quite specific in terms of what sort of movement to make which will result in an action that will affect the appropriate group of muscles. For the canoeist learning a support stroke, advice to press upwards with the knee opposite to the paddle in the water will bring a greater feeling of stability. For the skier, the tip to, "Press down with the outside big toe", will help the ski to turn more effectively than the usual, "bend zee knees". For the hill walker, "Put your feet down flat" or "get off your toes" or "push up with the heel instead of the ball of the foot" or "look for flat spots to place your feet" will bring relief. If there are no flat spots, "put your heel on small bumps or stones to lift it up and make the foot more horizontal". Negotiating an awkward move as when crossing a stream on stones, stepping across a gap or when moving up or down a rocky scramble, are similar situations where decisions have to be made about whether advice is enough. "Trust your feet" or "use that hold there" might suffice for some. But bellowing correct instructions to others may be quite inappropriate since a deeper level of emotional support may be needed such as, "take my hand" or "hold onto my rucksack strap" or

"I'm right behind you". Will getting out the rope intensify anxiety or relieve it? It may decrease the leader's but will it add to theirs?

It should be noted in passing that some leader training schemes have not paid a great deal of attention to the skills of teaching or coaching in the past. This has been the case because it was assumed understandably that the majority of people electing to do leader training were themselves either teachers or youth leaders. This may not necessarily remain true for the future. The imminence of national vocational qualifications (NVQs) for people wanting to work with groups out of doors will make career paths more accessible to individuals who are outside the two traditional public sector sources for recruitment to leader training. It will therefore become more necessary to lay a greater emphasis on teaching and coaching skills in schemes of training in order to maintain quality in leading and managing groups. This will be no bad thing in any case. It is often forgotten that whilst teachers and youth leaders may have been trained to teach, they are not likely to have been trained in the arts of coaching and teaching **physical** skills which, whilst there are some resemblances, is not quite the same thing. Quite different capacities and skills in the other hemisphere of the brain are entailed.

insight

One of a leader's most invaluable aids in coaching and supporting will be the **ability to recall past experience,** particularly feelings as a beginner. It will enable a leader to appreciate and to be more acutely aware that, if there are occasions now which are felt to be personally extending in the slightest bit, there will be some in the group in whom these feelings will be greatly magnified. This kind of recall whereby one is able to put oneself in another person's shoes, facilitates 'insight'. Probable examples are fearfulness when negotiating sections of rocky scrambling or narrow paths across steep slopes or steep descents, feelings of cold, hunger, thirst and fatigue to which a leader is more likely to be acclimatised than the group. Insight is partly

rooted in some degree of self awareness and sensitivity to others, but it can be developed by the frequent reflection and evaluation of personal experiences.
In recalling past experience to aid a coaching problem, it would be a mistake always to equate it with personal technical skill. The, "I found it easy, why can't you?" type of response is narrow and lacking in empathy.

It is the personal recollection of <u>feelings</u> at moments of great personal challenge or during times of stress, such as when very fatigued or frightened, that are of greater importance for leaders since they are the very foundation for empathy with others.

If such feelings of struggling and inadequacy have never been experienced by say, a very able and athletic leader, such a person will have to work very hard indeed to imagine what it feels like.

It will be remembered that in the section on risk, the perception of risk and its attendant feelings was seen to be an intensely personal thing which varies greatly in people. Leaders seeing youngsters faltering over a physical movement or skill should not hastily view it as a purely technical problem but recognise it as perhaps an emotional one requiring a very different set of responses from them. (see examples in the preceding section on 'supporting')

<u>problem solving - needs/wants - rules</u>

One of the things the leader of a group is often called upon to deal with is helping the group to come to terms with the conflict between its needs and its wants. What you want is not always what you need. A minibus group travelling from home to a distant campsite may want to stop at every motorway cafe they meet for a drink or snack. But they may need to arrive at the campsite early enough to avoid the difficulties of setting up camp in the dark in a strange place. A leader's task will be to help a group to understand and accept this. It will be just as important that the outcome is achieved without seriously impairing the leader - group relationships. It is very easy for a leader feeling the pressure of responsibility and able, from experience perhaps, to foresee the consequences of bad decisions, to override objections and protests and heavy handedly decide needs come before wants.

There are times when wants may have to come before needs, especially in the early history of a group, when to deny wants may so seriously affect relationships that it would be unwise to do so. Wants tend to be short-term and needs tend to be long-term in nature. But the denial of a short term want could be long term in its effect on relationships in a group !

Sometimes it is the needs of others quite outside the group that have to be considered. A classic example is after the end of camp with people neglecting or unwilling to do all the equipment maintenance jobs such as drying tents, cleaning utensils and crockery, repairing damage and replacing missing items. The next group to use the gear will need it to be serviceable. The current group may want to dash off now, because there is a special T.V. programme or an important local soccer match it wants to see now and leave everything for 'somebody' else to do. It is quite prepared to ignore the needs of some unknown group in the future. How a leader resolves these difficult choices will exercise a key influence on the future life of the group. It may even bring about its demise. To release the group unconditionally is a 'group win, leader lose' situation. To insist they stay is a 'leader win, group loses' situation. The ideal situation is where everybody wins. One possible solution would be for the leader and group to agree to disperse now, but promise to re-assemble at an agreed time in the future to complete the job.

The conflict between needs and wants is often entailed in the process of making rules to demarcate the limits of acceptable group behaviour.

The older the group, the more important is it to involve the group in the formulation of them. Detailed discussion about the need for a particular rule will ensure that at least everyone understands the reasons for it. Negotiation about the particular form a rule assumes is more likely ensure that it is observed. If it is not, then the group has to look at why and may become involved in a whole range of moral discoveries to do with trust, group loyalty, how to deal with disobedience, the nature of punishment and justice and so on - which is just as important for young people to know about as how to read a map or cope with moving water on a river. 'Doing' types may find this difficult to accept. But it is important to remember that, above all, one is teaching people not a subject.

judgement

Judgement involves the application of intelligence to a problem in order to collect certain information. This will be the specific, relevant information necessary to enable a correct decision to be made about selecting from many possibilities, the right course of action needed to solve the problem.

The skill of accurate judgement is greatly dependent upon the quality and quantity of past experience. But this experience-base is of limited value unless it has been processed in an internal reviewing procedure [21] which sifts, measures, analyses, synthesises, evaluates and draws conclusions from the facts of the experiences. It can be further enhanced by the creative use of the imagination to visualise situations where similar circumstances might exist in different permutations of degree or even sequence. Drawing up a critical path analysis for a developing situation is a roughly comparable example. These acts of processing provide a more conscious store of information in the memory from which to develop criteria and standards which are used to help estimate the value, nature and significance of conditions confronted at some time in the future. Information is required in this form to enable predictions about possible outcomes to be made.

Judgement is often a matter of comparing questions of degree. How closely does this compare with the last time? A simple example is when the map shows there are five kilometres still to walk which one can normally expect to take about an hour. But there are other factors present to be taken into account. There is a strong head wind, it is towards the end of the day, and the group is tiring. The memory is scanned for previous similar circumstances and similar groups to enable you to estimate how long it is likely to take this group to cover the distance. You judge it is going to be longer than you would like, and a short cut would help matters greatly. So, " If I took this short cut down here I could probably save half an hour. The angle of the slope is fairly steep and the group could probably manage it. But because of the angle of slope, the ground surface needs to give a good grip for the feet. From experience I know that bracken, tallish grass or a soft surface would help. But this is hard with very short turf and wet from that last shower. Nasty! I predict the consequences of trying to descend it could be greater than the problem I'm trying to solve. Better leave it" Or on another day, " There is no wind down here but I see those clouds up there are moving very fast. I remember noticing that once and finding it pretty wild on the tops. These clouds are moving even faster than that time. Maybe I should not take this group of beginners that high on their first trip out today." Or, " The last time we went sailing/canoeing with the waves that high, we were lucky to get back. And they were a good group - this is not. Better postpone it."

Judgement relies heavily on a person's ability to analyse situations. Present in any situation are hundreds of factors to be scanned and identified. The problem and the skill is to discern those factors whose effects will be the most significant in a chosen course of action. Skill in being able to correlate all such vital factors is also needed. No situation is ever exactly the same. Previous successful solutions will not necessarily prove viable again. The ability quickly to see why, is a great asset. It cannot be emphasised too strongly or often enough that the path to success in this area lies in frequent, conscientious reflection and evaluation of one's experiences. Becoming wiser after the event is a good way to develop a future sound, judgmental skill.

• The really difficult times are those when the leader is on the fringe of known experience, when previous experience is not much help. Being able to control feelings of insecurity and anxiety caused by the unknown or doubts is a definite requirement in leaders.

" The really difficult times are when the leader is on the fringe of known experience. "

Faced by something quite new or unknown, a leader may first have to screw down anxiety before the mind can begin to observe properly and apply the processes of induction, deduction and maybe intuition, to unzip possible causes, consequences and implications. A good imagination may even be of assistance here.

• Sometimes it is difficult beforehand to decide what kind of moral value to put on a course of action because it is in the sphere of bipolar values. By this I mean when the same action can be judged to be either foolhardy and reckless, or courageous and strong depending on the point of view. Another act can be either cautious and wise, or cowardly and weak. How does one decide which it is? The fear of being judged wrongly by others, or the desire to be judged fairly, is not to be lightly dismissed. Sometimes all there is to help is the integrity of personal inner resources and convictions - aims and goals again! Leaders have to be able to justify their actions articulately to themselves as well as others.

decision-making methods

Decisions stem from judgement and are meant to promote action to resolve problems or achieve aims.
Since leaders have to make decisions about how decisions are made, it will be useful to describe the various ways in which decisions can be made. In no order of priority they are:

-By authority without discussion: as when 'authority' makes a decree. It is quick and efficient for emergencies when time is short and speed important. But it may not be very effective if the group who has to implement the decision does not fully understand it or feel involved in it. Motivation is likely to be low or even non existent if they do not agree with it.

-By an expert member: who 'pronounces' a verdict or opinion. This may be fine for some situations but how do you tell who is the expert? In most outdoor situations where a technical problem is posed, it is likely to be the adult leading the young people who has the technical expertise. But in a peer group as found with Award expedition groups it is not so obvious. Popularity may be substituted for expertise. Individuals with power tend to overestimate their expertise. With a group of adults the leader may be obvious providing it is a technical problem, but if non technical matters are the issue, confusion may arise as to where decision making power lies. But overall, this method is better than the next one.

-By an average of members' opinions: this is rather like majority voting. A straw poll is taken to find the popular view . The most common opinion is unlikely to be in the majority. Also the best opinion may be cancelled out by an ignorant or uninformed view. Because opinions are not allowed to interact and modify each other, decision making is likely to be of a low order. Motivation and commitment, despite apparent consultation will be poor too.

-By authority after discussion: since the leader initiates the process in calling a meeting to present a problem requiring solution, the group is aware that a rough decision has already been made and that the function of their contribution is merely to approve or modify it slightly. The final decision will still be made by the leader so the sense of involvement is weak. Leaders using this method need to be good listeners in order that the eventual decision benefits fully from what the group says. Members may also try to impress the leader or tell him what they think s/he wants to hear.

-By majority control: this is such a common, taken-for-granted feature in our society that it is used thoughtlessly without a real understanding of the implications of the 'numbers game' that is being played when the winner is the 51% 'first past the post' or the sub group with most votes. The most win but many lose. It is sometimes even a minority which makes the decision. The classic example being the

Referendum voting which propelled the UK into the European Community in the early 1970s when the total of 'don't knows' and 'against' was greater than the 'yeas'. Unlike the electoral system however, in this method, minority opinions are not always respected and may be brow beaten by the winners. 'Yes/No' thinking is raised to a too sacred level, to the point that it creates blindness, irrational, polarised argument and discourages the consideration of viable alternatives. As a method for deciding rules where it is important that everyone agrees, it is patently unsuitable. Effective majority decision making requires that everyone feels they had a fair hearing.

-By minority control: in which a sub group such as a committee is given authority to decide. This is useful when there is not enough time to shift a lot of business or when the consequences are not too serious if poor decisions are made. But there are risks that only the decision makers are committed to the course of action and resistance from the rest may be passive or positively active. This type of decision making also occurs when a powerful sub group attempts to 'railroad' through a proposition. The manner of the railroading not only denies people enough time to think, but may make some afraid to speak out against it. The danger then is that silence is read as consent whereas in reality, silence develops into a form of underground resistance.

-By consensus: a thorough ventilation of the problem and all points of view about it, permits the group to reach a point that is agreeable to all. i.e. all win. This is the most effective method for decision making which involves the resolution of conflicts and controversies, but it is time consuming and requires a high degree of member skill and energy. High quality decisions ensue from this method.
Since all are fully involved, the degree of motivation and commitment to carry out the decision is high. Duke of Edinburgh Award groups, for example, consisting of peers, would find the consensus method of decision making perhaps best suited to their situation when on expedition.

group decision-making

Group decision making confers benefits which are absent when only a single person is making a decision. There is an exchange and use of a greater diversity of information and hence a stimulation of new thoughts.

There is likely to be increased motivation since the weaker members will tend to imitate and compare themselves with peers felt to be of higher ability.

There is a feeling of more support and encouragement than when on one's own. Members will feel a greater accountability to the others, therefore group loyalty will increase.

There is more motivation to rethink if one meets disagreement with one's own view. The processing of information whereby it is rehearsed and elaborated increases its meaning, facilitates comprehension, imparts a deeper level of understanding and aids its retention.

Insight is gained into a variety of ways in which to view the decision.

Security of numbers creates a willingness to adopt more extreme or dynamic positions than would an individual alone.

But it is as well to remember that good decisions depend on how effective the group is. The quality of their relationships, which largely depends on how much respect they have for each other and how much tolerance and trust there is amongst them, will affect their ability to communicate well, resolve conflicts and disagreements, define goals and agree on a course of realistic action to achieve them.

An effective decision is one where:

-time and the resources of the whole group are fully used;
-the decision is implemented fully by all the group or those designated;
-the future problem solving ability of the group is not inhibited by further sets of grievances or problems created by the present decision.

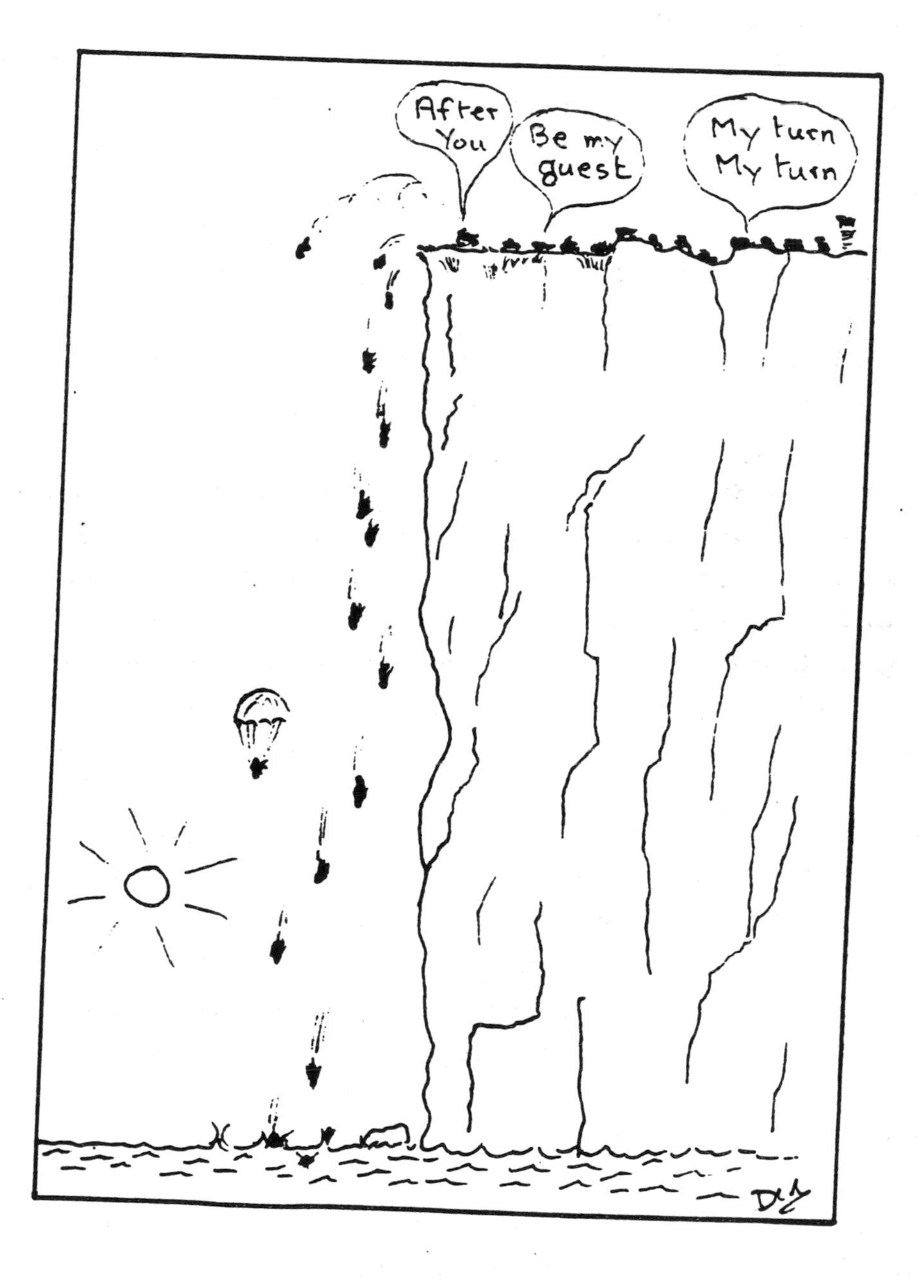

" Security of numbers creates a willingness to adopt more extreme or dynamic positions."

factors hindering group decision-making

Whilst there are many advantages to be derived from group decision making it is as well to be aware of certain negative aspects relating to group decision making which will minimise those benefits. Here is a brief review of them.

- If the group has only had a short time to get to know each other, this will reduce the degree of group maturity. It is after the passing of the 'storming' phase that groups tend to mature and work more effectively.

- When the personal goals of members conflict with those of the group, this will slow down, impoverish the decision or even prevent it. When such goals are undeclared they are known as 'hidden agendas' and may or may not thus sabotage the group's efforts, cause conflict or disruption. Hidden agendas are always present and should be accepted as legitimate - not to be complained about or scolded for. Consensus agreement about group goals would help avoid this sort of negative situation.

- The failure of individuals, because of shyness, laziness or reluctance, to participate equally, or their inability to communicate well, listen and use information will cause resentment, disharmony or suspicion.

- Self centred outlooks of members unable to step outside the limits of their own prejudices and attitudes will cause side issues to arise which will conflict with, and detract attention from, more serious matters.

- Pressure sometimes comes from individuals to reach agreement too quickly or prematurely. This may take the form of compromises pushed too early before there has been time for a realistic appraisal of a problem; or seeking solutions before the problem is understood; or the quick suppression of disagreement or the stifling of discussion which might give rise to possible conflict.

• An insufficient diversity of types of people will not provide the desirable and necessary variety of skills and outlooks for a richer, wider interaction.

• Those unskilled in the art of discussion will experience interference with, or blocking of, their contributions to discussion because they are unable to find a slot for it at the right time. Ground rules for holding and taking part in a discussion may be needed.

• Groups larger than eight or nine will tend to be held in thrall by the dominant ones. Inappropriate group size will gravitate against the involvement of everyone.

• Many groups have in-built power structures that have appeared early in the group's life. These cause power differences between members. When this occurs, fear, defensiveness and distrust inhibit frank and open exchange.

time requirements for decisions

Group processes also take quite a lot of time so there needs to be as much time as a particular task of decision making requires to be properly carried through. The size of the group affects the process too; the bigger the group, the more time is needed.
Diagram 7. illustrates the concept[14].

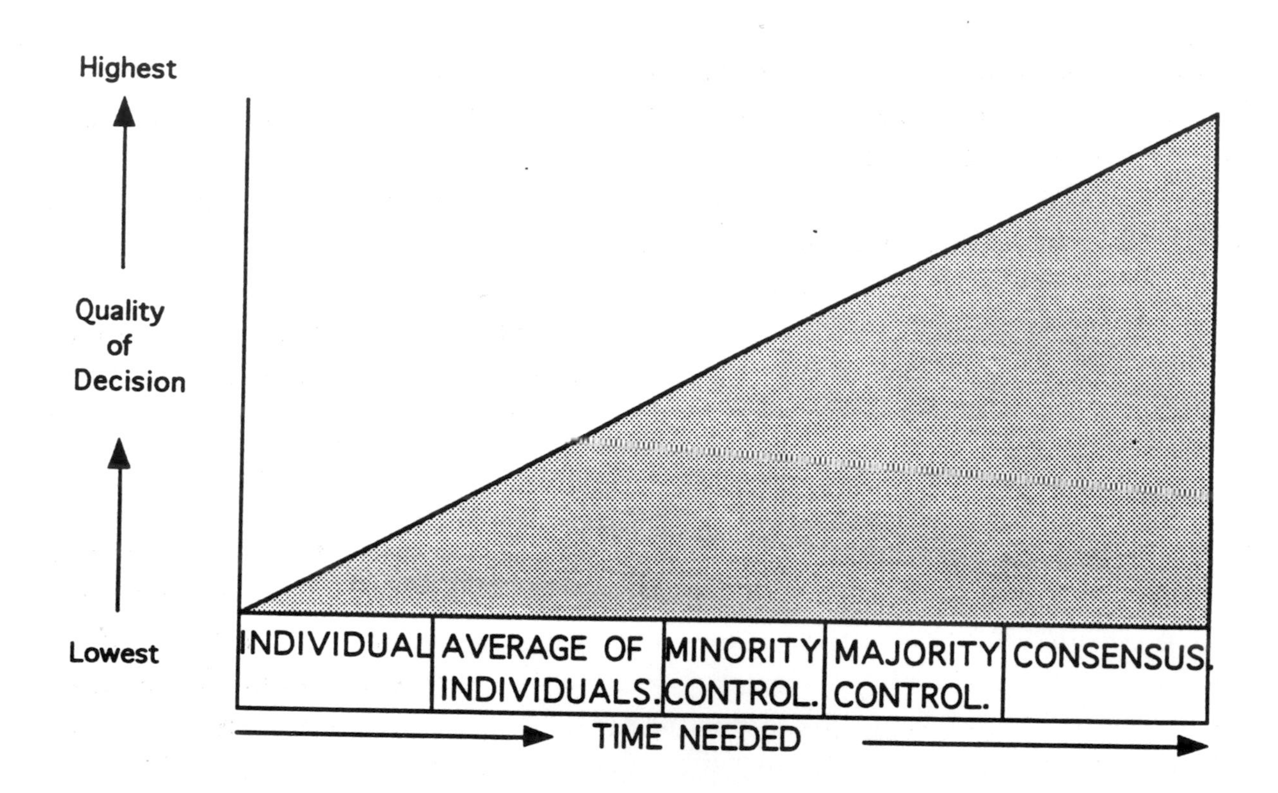

Diagram: 7. Time requirement related to the number making the decision.

skill and practice for group decision-making

Good decision-making by groups is only feasible when members possess the necessary skills and motivation to work collaboratively, which means they must be able to communicate effectively and manage conflicts constructively and not sabotage group efforts. Leaders of groups of young people should be aware that these skills do not arrive overnight and that like every other skill, they require practice. Young groups learning these skills will make plenty of mistakes as they fumble towards competence in this arena. So leaders will need lots of patience and understanding as they witness much frustration in the group and must be quite convinced about the value of time spent learning decision making. Leaders may be tempted to wait until the group is more mature before permitting group participation in these

important functions. It is so easy to say that the time is not yet right. But when will the time ever be right for acquiring this important skill? The answer has to be that the time must nearly always be right.
A good leader will normally try to get the group participating in as many decisions as is consistent with safety, and as is compatible with their age and ability. For example, the group could be given the chance to say what sort of things they would like to see or do on a particular day. Leaders too often think they know best and maybe sometimes they do. But people of any age like to feel that they have discovered or decided some things for themselves.

A group of remedial youngsters were quite determined in their desire to be in dinghies on Lake Windermere on a day so wild and windy that the staff had already written off sailing in the programme for the day. But these youngsters would not be shifted from their aim. Continuing good relationships required some kind of 'all win' compromise to be found. The eventual answer was to allow the group to row the dinghies in the lee of a convenient headland. Whenever the dinghies began to drift into wilder water, the safety boat towed them back into calmer waters to carry on. Staff on their own would never have dreamed up such a day believing it to be too low a level of involvement. The youngsters had a great day and got a lot from it.

Feedback from group planning sessions are invaluable to the leader in providing insight into the level of student aspiration and ambition and of what they think they are capable. This may not be as feasible with some novice groups. But much can be done by skillful prompting to help them identify their expectations and feel involved. Often when people are asked what they want to do, they just do not know. It is necessary to spell out in some detail the choices that are available. It is rather like dressing a shop window. One of the outdoor leader skills is to be able to identify for a novice group, a choice of objectives in such a way that degrees of challenge and/or attractiveness are readily apparent: "Would you like to visit a small lake surrounded by trees and bushes halfway up a hill today, or scramble up a rocky ravine with a stream running down it, or walk to reach a high rocky summit with great views?" When alternatives are involved, it is a shrewd move to itemise the implications of a particular choice or course of action because it is probable that coming to them 'cold', the group will not have had time to realise the consequences such as the amount of preparation needed, or the time required to do it or the effort it will entail.

"The youngsters had a great day and got a lot out of it."

More experienced groups are quite likely to have ideas about what they want to do which will be useful, not only for gearing up their sense of commitment, but for providing the leader, often incidentally, with feedback on their assessment of themselves.

'Dressing the shop window' has useful applications in other situations. For example, when faced by setbacks or minor disasters many youngsters do not really know how to respond, so they react. All they have to rely on are their gut reactions which are more than likely to be unproductive. A leader can help everyone at a crucial time in providing the needed information. This would be by pointing out the various ways that are open to them to respond to a situation and asking which one it is going to be. Positive choices are usually made when the information base is comprehensive.

When some of the tents blow down, group members have the choice of blaming each other or the leader for not checking properly, blaming the wind which won't listen and anyway the wind that did it is miles away now, blaming the pegs for bending or pulling out, or if they ever hope to spend a comfortable night, making the best of a bad job by pitching in (no pun intended) to re-erect the tents as quickly as possible. If they finish their own tent soon, is it better to scramble into it out of the wind and wet or instead help others less fortunate to complete theirs first.

This was a real life situation and the decision making that resulted from laying out the choice of alternatives before them was very surprising and pleasing. Often for young people, the choices are not obvious until pointed out.

general note on quality of decision-making

What makes a high or low quality decision is fine in theory, but in the real world we are not often in possession of all the facts; we are not usually aware of all the good or bad consequences of our decisions; we are not as rational as we would like to think either, because our decisions are often based on rationalisations of emotional stances which decided the way we would go before we even realised it; we are rarely sure of the rightness of a decision and are usually worried or doubtful about it; we often look for the line of least resistance, the answer that will cause least trouble/upset or have minimal impact or the solution that requires least effort and resources so is the most easily carried out; we sometimes prefer to do nothing because change creates a fearful uncertainty about the future and so we carry on regardless as before; sometimes, by contrast, we hope a change might work a miracle and opt for it without really comprehending the consequences; if we are faced with a number of unattractive alternatives we are likely to feel that we are damned if we do and damned if we don't, so we waste time, put it off, delay, pass the buck, anything to avoid the stress of the controversial decision. The 'down' side of consensus decision making is that in trying to design a horse one might end up with a camel !

objective versus group

One of the difficult major planning decisions to resolve always is whether the make-up of a group should be determined by the nature of the objective such as a designated hill, or whether the nature of that hill to be climbed, its distance, height, roughness, remoteness, should be determined by the structure of the group, the number of members in it, their age, experience, skill and ability. Do you only recruit/select the few elite performers to accompany you on a difficult journey?. If the number of members in the group are many, do you reduce them for a testing objective? If the characteristics of the group are very variable, do you take them all but select an objective within the capacity of the lowest denominator? Since the variety and range of objectives or challenges available for choice is almost infinite and since the members who present themselves to form a group is often largely predetermined, there should not be much doubt about which alternative to adopt.

Other outdoor activities have their own particular type of "hill" to deal with. A river to be canoed will be assessed for its remoteness, access points, length, general water speed, roughness and frequency of rapids, clear or obstructed banks. A ski slope will be scrutinised for its steepness, the depth, texture and condition of the snow, open or restrictive spaces for manoeuvring, density of other skiers and so on.

It is usually much easier to match the challenge to the group than it is to match the group to the challenge. Group discussion about the objective for the day should facilitate the resolution of this problem in the early stages of planning. During any journey over land or water, there are many decisions in which the group should be encouraged to participate such as, when to stop for lunch, where to go next, identifying landmarks, who navigates next or takes the helm, and even whether to go on or not.

crisis management

But it is the emergency/crisis decisions that are the particular province and concern of the leader. If the skills and habits already outlined have been developed strongly enough, the business of personal decision making by the leader should be half accomplished already. For the big important decisions relating to the group's safety, the relevant factors will have been already observed or anticipated. It is then a question of using past experience to assess all the factors for and against, and picking out the best course of action from a number of possible alternatives.
Emergencies are a special case however.

Managing an emergency situation, 'crisis management' as it is sometimes called, is a good example of a 'frontier' experience referred to earlier. If it occurs suddenly and unexpectedly in the form of an accident, it will be an unusual leader who does not experience some shock. The mind is numbed temporarily and this paralysis can induce a form of panic caused by the fear of not living up to the expectation of being the leader who always knows what to do. This is followed by a mass of unrelated, half-baked plans, courses of action, ideas, facts and figures flooding the brain that can compound the feeling of helplessness. Leaders should be comforted by the knowledge that this is a normal reaction to the situation. By keeping calm and waiting for the surge to pass, as pass it will, rather than going off at half cock too early, a lot of distress will be avoided all round. There is an admirable piece of advice from the States for this situation, "Don't just do something, sit there". Obviously if blood is pumping all over the place or breathing has stopped, urgent, immediate action is required. The difficult part is arriving at a workable plan to evacuate the patient. By the time ten, even thirty, seconds have elapsed, which may feel like ten minutes, you should be in a sufficiently calm state to be able to think more clearly and get on with sorting the myriad of detail into an organised plan of action.

Even if the emergency has developed slowly, the realisation that you have one on your hands is likely to be sudden and the effect on you similar to a surprise accident. A depth of previous experience will be of tremendous help in the formulation of answers to the problems posed by the situation.

Thus we return again to the quality of this all important previous personal experience. Learn about your personal limitations in your chosen activity before ever leading parties. Get to know not only the inner self, but how the self is in various technical emergency-type situations, for example, beware against anxiety causing undue haste whilst navigating in mist on land or fog at sea. Learn beforehand what it feels like to be lost temporarily; what it is like to be out in foul conditions; how to handle different types of terrain both in ascent and descent in the different seasons or varying conditions of wind and water; what it is like to be out at night. Try a planned bivouac.

reviewing and its benefits

"We had the experience but missed the meaning." T.S.Eliot.

Whilst there are leaders these days who take groups on an outdoor activity with the single-minded aim of doing it purely for its own sake, most leaders have some broader aim in view to facilitate the personal development of each group member in some way. This sub-section is relevant to such aspirations.

Reference has been made already to the benefits that a leader can enjoy from looking back over an experience in order to extract important lessons from it. It cannot be repeated too often that the adoption and exercising of this practice regularly, is one of the best aids to self improvement that the leader can have. It helps develop insight and judgmental skills. Very often there are other lessons to be learned which do not become obvious until an experience has been reflected upon. If it can not be retained in the memory to be easily recalled when necessary, it is lost learning. Reflection guided by a structured process (see below) facilitates the degree of retention and improves the quality of what is retained.
Most leaders are probably familiar with the increasing degree of impact that the auditory, visual, and performance styles of communication are said to have on memory and learning, " To hear is to forget, to see is to remember, to do is to understand". But like all generalisations there can be exceptions to this hierarchy of learning. People tend to have a preferred 'learning medium'. Some learn better through the auditory rather than visual and vice versa. But it is likely that more enduring learning takes place when people are living and participating in an experience. Then all the capacities of the thinking, doing, feeling self are more engaged because they are more comprehensively involved and in an integrated way. This is illustrated by the quotation "All learning is experiential, but some learning is more experiential than others." 22

Whilst some of our learning has to be received second hand through normal directive and didactic, teaching methods, much has to be learned for ourselves heuristically - by experiencing and discovering it.

The experiential learning process is distinguished by having four main components:-
-planning;
-execution and action;
-reflection;
-application.

Experiences are only special if we think about them in order to make them personal to ourselves. We do that to discover what was important or significant about them and what may be of future usefulness.

Members of the group will benefit, no less than the leader, from this kind of process. But beware of over doing it lest the group become bored or alienated by too frequent exposure to it. To get the best out of it however, it should be preplanned to ensure that there is adequate time for it and most importantly, to give the group fair and advance notice. To spring a review session unexpectedly on a group is to invite all manner of brickbats !

a suggested model for reviewing

Reviewing should be properly structured by having a conceptual model on which to base one's ideas about how to organise and proceed in such a session. One useful model follows a sequence of levels of thinking which progress from the simplest to the more complex. These levels are:

1. Knowledge - which is the memory level: remembering facts by recognition or recall.
2. Comprehension - which is the understanding level: explaining or interpreting knowledge in a descriptive way- knowing why and how.
3. Application - which is the usage level: using knowledge correctly.
4. Analysis - which is the relationship level: breaking down knowledge and perceiving relationships between the parts.

5. Synthesis- which is the creative level: putting bits together to make a whole.
6. Evaluation- which is the opinion level: forming opinions, making judgements about the value of ideas, solutions, events.

The point about this structure is that information on a particular level is not accessible to a person until the previous level has been adequately dealt with. To ask for an opinion (level 6) before syntheses (level 5) have been made is futile. You can't build a ceiling if you have no walls. So experiences have to be 'processed' in an orderly manner to gain maximum advantage from them.
A commonly used shorthand device to aid the memorisation of this process is:

- What?
- So what?
- Now what?

The 'action' orientated leader, or indeed the group, who may feel this exercise of the brain is pointless, needs to ask the question, "Is it more important to experience much or is it more important to make meaning out of that which is experienced?" It is possible to have had a lot of experience but have learned very little from it. It would be possible for example to keep making the same mistakes and be blithely unaware of it, locked as it were, in a cycle of innocent incompetence.

Reviewing bestows a number of benefits. In the process of looking at the sequence of events ('what did you do'?), and the various processes (how and why did you do it?) such as consulting, negotiating or decision making and the part played by individuals, much valuable feedback can be generated which, provided it is of the right, positive kind, will result in improvements in motivation, self awareness, relationships, group unity and performance (how do you feel about it?). Reflection is conducive to insight.

" A cycle of innocent incompetence"

The leader's ability to generate a caring climate of trust and cooperation is very necessary to successful reviewing. The aggressive, competitive, point-scoring atmosphere characteristic of some male behaviour needs to be discouraged since this would severely disrupt the chances of positive results.

<u>recording</u>

Allied to the reviewing process is the practice and skill of writing down and recording events, experiences and thoughts as another aid to the leader's self improvement.
It is very easy to jumble up sequences of events when trying to recall them. Changing the order in which they occur can impart quite a different meaning or interpretation to them - in the context of group conflicts or misunderstandings this can be crucial.
It is very easy to be deceived later after the event into thinking that predictions and expectations turned out exactly as it was anticipated and judged they would, or that the results or consequences of decisions were what it was intended they would be. If they had been written down beforehand the difference might be very surprising. Recording keeps leaders firmly grounded in reality !

Some events can't always be explained immediately. Recording means there is an opportunity to keep working on them. The act of writing besides requiring the sorting out of the material into an orderly manner also reinforces the process whereby events are imprinted on memory. But to be successful, recording requires an act of personal commitment and much self discipline for it is not the most attractive of tasks.

<u>communication skills</u>

Communication is a four stage process in which everyone sends-receives-interprets- and infers. There is no set order in which these functions occur; indeed they usually happen simultaneously. Effective communication takes place between a 'sender' and a 'receiver' when the receiver interprets a message in the way that the sender intended it to be understood. Communication can be affected by 'interference' either at the sender's end, (sender's attitude, frame of reference, appropriateness of speech such as very long words or swearing or coarseness) or at the receiver's end, (receiver's attitudes, prejudices, background, experiences that affect the decoding process) or certain kinds of 'noise' in between the two people communicating (environmental sounds, speech problems such as a mumble, stammer, or distracting mannerisms.

Communication is the basis for all human interaction and group working. Every group must take in and use information. The very existence of the group depends on communication. Set in this context, the leader's ability to communicate effectively is crucial since it is the all-pervading means by which leadership is delivered or exercised. So clearly the quality of leadership can be greatly affected by the quality of the communication skills possessed by a leader.
Whilst actions do speak louder than words, and leading by conscious example is important in many ways, it is as well to remember that leaders can lead by unconscious example, in that non verbal communication, which has already been mentioned as a means of detecting signals from the group, also works in reverse - groups pick up the leader's non verbals and very quickly !

But for most of the time it is the spoken word which permeates everything, whether it is giving information, issuing instructions, selling an idea, recommending a course of action, helping to resolve a conflict or knowing when to be silent (of which more anon). It is necessary to be aware that it is not just the 'content' of what is said that is important but the emotional tone with which it is delivered. A telling off is more likely to be received if it is delivered in a neutral tone than one in which the voice is perceived to be scolding, nagging, whining, angry, censorious or indignant (but paradoxically with some people, a reasonable tone does not work and it is sometimes only an emotional message that gets through to register). It is quite possible for a statement to be made in which the tone of voice absolutely contradicts the intent of what is being said. This is called a 'crossed message'. Sarcasm is a good example of this. "Please do take your time" can be said with an inflection that means quite the opposite. It is important to ensure that the 'emotional message' matches the message content.

It is vital to express oneself positively. It is helpful to avoid the use of 'always' in the manner "you always do that" (no one 'always' does anything). Refrain from an over-use of negatives (don't do that; you can't do this; that's no good at all!) which so often cause feelings of frustration and resentment.

It is vital to express oneself clearly. Try to avoid loose or careless expression in the spoken delivery. Even when you are trying hard to be positive and clear, be aware that there are many opportunities for being wrongly interpreted. What means one thing to person A, will mean something quite different to person B. Heedless, thoughtless ways of expressing yourself can mislead the listener. Leaders can check if a wrong image or impression has been presented by resorting to a system of feedback. To check out what has been received ask one of the group to play back by re-stating to you what they think you have said. This also gives an opportunity, that would otherwise not have arisen, to clarify misunderstandings or correct any misinterpretation.

<u>listening</u>

Since communicating with others is a two-way process, the ability to express oneself by 'sending', is only a half of the story. It is equally important to be able to 'receive' or listen properly. Good listening is an art, a skill and a discipline and not the simple process it is usually conceived to be. It is possible to listen, but not hear what is said. It is possible to hear, but not understand, or even misunderstand, what is said. Hearing only becomes listening when close attention is paid to what is said.

How often in the middle of listening to someone, when you hear something you do not agree with, do you apparently keep listening, but in fact shut off whilst you begin to marshal the elements of your counter argument? (On-off listening).
How often listening to some boring account, does your head continue to nod and make all the minor signals of receiving, when in fact you could not afterwards repeat any of it? (Glassy-eyed listening).
How often when you hear something that seems to oppose the very essence of your being or some important value held dear, do you get so angry you tune out and stop listening? (Red flag listening).
How often do you conclude too quickly that you know what is coming and decide there is no further reason to continue listening? (Open ears-closed mind listening).

Good listening requires an emotional, intellectual and behavioural control that comes only with effort and practice. Good and careful listening can be astonishingly energy-draining. In a group it is important that people talk freely about matters and problems that are important to them. The more information a leader has about these matters, the better the leader will be able to know how to go about dealing with them effectively. This is where knowing when to be silent is a leader's priceless asset. Then there will be a minimum of leader-initiated argument, interruption, unwanted advice, premature judgments and hasty conclusions, all of which are barriers to good listening.
Silence can be taken too far however, to the point where it inhibits interaction. So silence used to minimise negative communication must be complemented by 'noise(s)' to show interest, understanding and empathy with the speaker(s) e.g. "that's interesting, I see, uh-huh, geez, wow, crikey", and so on as appropriate.

<u>silence</u>

There are times when silence can be used deliberately as a means of extracting a response when one is needed. But it should be used with caution. Most people react uneasily to silence and will try to fill it, not necessarily with what you are looking for. If the silence rebounds on the leader by becoming protracted and very 'heavy', this may be because the group do not yet understand what is being asked of them. The exact nature of the problem they are being asked to solve or a decision they are expected to make, may not have occurred to them yet. Quite often the group too will use silence to exact an answer from the leader who must then attempt to discern whether they are too lazy, tired or bored to exert themselves because each of those conditions requires a different kind of response.

Communication as an art and skill is a very big subject and all that can be attempted here is a little to whet the appetite for more. It is inadvisable to think that what skill you have is quite adequate. In this particular area of human activity there is always room for improvement, especially for those who would lead others successfully.

meta skills

We saw earlier that skills may be classified in many ways. Some skills seem to be fairly simple and are quickly acquired; others are more complex, not as easily learned, not as easily mastered, if ever. Once you learn how to tie a bowline knot for example, that is it. Or is it? There is more to learn about it for there are two or three other ways of tying it. Thereafter, there is nothing more to learn about the actual business of how to tie the knot, but you could go on to learn many different applications for the knot and the circumstances in which it can be used. This so called 'climber's knot' is much used by sailors, for example. The ability to use a skill in a number of different ways is one form of the skill of versatility and the example of the knot was a very elementary way of illustrating the point.

A similar sort of higher level process applies to the use of relationship skills. As knowledge, awareness and understanding grows about various aspects of group behaviour, it becomes possible to work on more than one level at a time. The process can be likened to 'multi-tasking',

which is the way a more advanced computer is able to do a number of jobs simultaneously. You can be paying attention to the content of what individuals in the group are saying (one level) whilst monitoring the non-verbal effect on the whole group (second level) and at the same time, be using this in-coming information to decide whether an intervention from you is necessary or not (third level). Above all this (fourth level), you could also be trying to make an overall evaluation of what is going on, i.e. how worthwhile is it to spend time on this, are lessons being learned, does it help the group to move on to achieve its objective or is it leading to disruption?
This kind of multi-activity is of a higher order of skill which may be called a 'meta skill'. It is a fairly sophisticated skill which takes time to acquire and can only be used in short bursts as it uses a lot of energy.

the skill of using skills

There is another skill which can be included in the 'meta' category. It is based on discretion and discrimination, to match up the use of particular leadership techniques to the right person or group, at the right time, in the right place for the right reason or job to be done. If a wood chisel for example, is used as a screw driver, the end result will be imperfect. There is a risk of damage both to the tool and the material being worked on. In a similar way it is possible for a person to be technically highly proficient but still be quite inadequate as a leader because of an inability to relate to people and a tendency to mismatch 'people' skills. This may be either because s/he does not want to, or because s/he does not know how, or because personal qualities are such as to make it unlikely that s/he ever will. The sensitivity with which all these skills are used greatly affects the way they are used and therefore the effect that they will have in a group. Technical skill in a leader without the seasoning of human understanding has little value. Without this sophistication to inform his/her actions it is possible for the most technically, highly qualified leader to give the group a negative experience.

Getting leadership right is a never-ending task. It is alive and ever-changing, whereas the purely technical is inanimate and relatively static. There are rarely neat answers or solutions. Situations will elicit from leaders, responses they never knew they had. Therein lies some of the fascination.

Do not be afraid of making mistakes - we all manage to do that every day. But have a positive attitude about them. Mistakes are about learning not about feeling guilty or being punished. That applies to the group as well as to the leader. Let them know this too and a lot of suppressed initiative will be released. The thing is to have good intentions, more especially conscious intentions allied to sound convictions. It helps to make intentions known in order to reduce the probability of being judged by the effects of your actions-especially when they go wrong. If mistakes in relationships are made they can be rectified, but it is necessary to know, or to have worked out, how to do that and repair any emotional damage. If such mistake-mending is neglected, hurts and resentments stack up to erode the leader's standing and credibility.

Some leaders feel it is unprofessional ever to admit to making mistakes. "Professionals do not make mistakes, only amateurs do that". To admit to such vulnerability would be to breach the infallible aura that they think should surround them.

On the subject of mistakes, it is amazing what a simple thing like a sincere apology will do to mend relationships. It does not cost much, but it buys a lot.

Outdoor leaders being the only adult in the group, may tend to feel awkward or downright resistant about apologising to young people out of a belief that it might undermine their authority or that it will place the leader at their mercy. Nothing could be further from the truth. Leaders tend to be seen by their groups as people who know what they are doing, where they are going and who know many of the answers. Groups become very troubled when the evidence seems to contradict this belief. Feeling troubled causes trouble. Leaders need sometimes to burst the bubble of infallibility perceived by groups to be around leaders. An apology sincerely made and sincerely meant will often be the way to show young people that adults have their limitations too and are not as different, inhuman, unapproachable or unreachable as was thought. Humility is an asset.

One could almost be excused for thinking that apologising is a meta skill too because it is felt to be so difficult. Subjective obstacles are the most difficult of all challenges to overcome. To reach an apology, it is sometimes necessary to be able to overcome a deep-rooted attitude or a strong emotion in order to acquire the humility that makes it possible.

concluding remarks

Many of the skills touched on in this essay should have been explored in greater detail, but space does not permit a full and comprehensive coverage here. For now, it is sufficient that the attention of aspirant leaders has been drawn to them. They are mostly the skills which contribute to the quality of working relationships in the leader-group situation: the art of dealing with and relating to people; the skills and intricacies of communication and listening; dealing with conflict; the relieving of tension, using humour; roles in groups; understanding the dynamics of group life and encouraging the full development of the individuals in your group; fostering self sufficiency, confidence and self determination in people.

For most of the group, the aim for the day may well be in getting to the top or the end and enjoying the experience. Whilst a leader's more basic responsibilities, in order of priority, will be the safety, comfort and enjoyment of the members of the group, they should feel it happening in exactly the reverse order for most of the time. It is often said that, "It is better to journey than to arrive". In this respect hopefully, leaders will be aware that there are many times when the processes of group interaction is just as important as the achievement of the aim.

Leaders, with an informed and more liberal interpretation of their role and a broader awareness of the potential of the outdoors as a marvellous medium for helping people to develop their capacities to the full, will be able to provide the atmosphere, the context and the setting for this to take place whilst taking care to remember in this day and age to minimise environmental damage.

"We shall not cease from exploration
And the end of all our exploring
Will be to arrive where we started
And know the place for the first time".

T.S.Eliot, -"Four Quartets".

References:

1 Outdoor Education-Safety and Good Practice. Guidelines for guidelines:pg12-15. Pub by Duke of Edinburgh Award.

2 R.A. Hogan.1992-Journal of Adventure Education and Outdoor Leadership (JAEOL) Vol.9:No.1. The Natural Environment in Wilderness Programmes. Playing Field or Sacred Place?

3 Mary Cox-1983. Leadership. MLTB 1983 Conference, Ripon.

4 John Adair-1983. Effective leadership; a self development manual: Gower Press.

5 A.H. Maslow- 1954. Motivation and personality. Harper & Row

6 R. Tannenbaum and W. Schmidt-1968. How to choose a leadership pattern: Harvard review.

7 P. Hersey and K.H. Blanchard-1969. Management of organisational behaviour.

8 R. Chase & S. Priest- 1989. (JAEOL) Vol.6:No.2. The conditional theory of outdoor leadership style.

8 T. Dixon & S. Priest-1991. Vol.8:No.1. Confirmation of the Conditional Outdoor Leadership Theory.

9 B.W. Tuckman-1965. Development sequence in small groups: Psychological Bulletin.

10 K.C. Ogilvie-1974. Dare to Live-a philosophy for outdoor education: Unpublished.

11 G. Rattray Taylor-1972. Re-think. Pelican Books

12 D. Morris-Manwatching.

13 Eric Berne. MD-1964. Games people play. Penguin.

14 D.W. Johnson-F.P. Johnson.-1987. Joining together. Group theory and Group Skills. Prentice-Hall.

15 K.C. Ogilvie-1985. Adventure Activities-a perspective view. Report by Sports Council for Northern Ireland of Adventure Activities Conference at Runkerry Outdoor Centre.

16 K.C. Ogilvie-1989. The management of risk. JAEOL. Vol.6:No.4.

17 R.D. Laing-1970. Knots. Penguin.

18 Article in "The Independent" 17/10/91 about the trial of Clarence Thomas in the U.S.A.

19 Dr. John Nicholson - Men and women: How different are they?

20 S. Priest - 1988. (JAEOL) Vol.5:No.1.Preparing Effective Outdoor Pursuit Leaders(PEOPL)

21 S. Priest-1990. JAEOL. Vol.7:No.3. Everything you always wanted to know about judgement, but were afraid to ask.

22 L.K. Quinsland & A. Van Ginkel-Summer-1988. JAEOL. Vol.5:No.3. How to process experience.

Sources for further reading:

- Various-1988. Journal of Adventure Education and Outdoor Leadership.(JAEOL)
  Vol.5:No.1. S.Priest - Outdoor Leadership around the World.
  S.Priest - Bibliography for outdoor leadership.
  J.Hunt - Ethics in Leader Training Models.
- K.C.Ogilvie-1985. JAEOL.Vol:2.No.4/5. Planning an Adventure Experience in the Outdoors.
- S. Priest-1988.-JAEOL. Vol:5.No.3. Avalanche-Decision analysis.
- D. Hammerman & S. Priest-1989. JAEOL. Vol.6:No.2. The enquiry/discovery approach to learning in Outdoor Education.
- S. Priest-1989. JAEOL. Vol.6:No.4. Teaching outdoor adventure skills.
- R. Chase & S. Priest-1990. JAEOL. Vol.7:No.1. Effective communication.
- Groundwork- Creative Reviewing.
- R. Greenaway-1991.JAEOL. Vol.9:No.2. Reviewing by Doing.
- M. Cox-1984. Facilitative Intervention in Adventure Activities. NAOE Conference Report 1984.
- D. Johnson.-1990. JAEOL. Vol:7.No.3. Women in the outdoors.
- B.Humberstone & P.Lynch.1991. JAEOL.Vol.8.No.3. Girls concepts of themselves and their experiences in outdoor education programmes.
- Abi Paterson-1989. Gender Issues: Case study of a Women's Leadership Course. NAOE Occasional Publications:No 4.
- S.Priest-1987-Preparing Effective Outdoor Pursuit Leaders. University of Oregon Press.
- S. Priest-1991. JAEOL.Vol:8.No.3. The Ten Commandments of Adventure Education.
- T.A. Harris.-1973. I'm O.K.-You're O.K. Pan Books Ltd.
- C.M. Steiner.-1975. Scripts people live. (transactional analysis of life scripts.) Bantam Books.
- M. James & D. Jongeward.1971. Born to win. (transactional analysis). Addison-Wesley Pub. Co.